To Rodney —

An orange-blood thoroughbred! May the Eyes of Texas always be upon you, and may life be good to you!

Hook 'em!

Margaret Berry

November 14, 1985 —

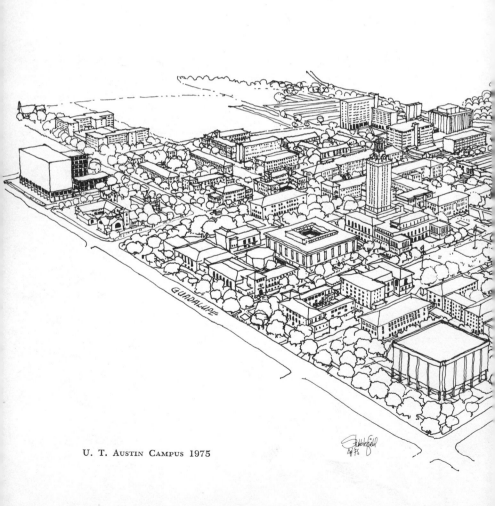

U. T. Austin Campus 1975

UT Austin

TRADITIONS AND
NOSTALGIA

UT Austin
TRADITIONS AND NOSTALGIA

BY
MARGARET CATHERINE BERRY

FIRST EDITION 1975
SECOND EDITION 1977
THIRD EDITION 1980

TEXT ILLUSTRATIONS BY
JOE STUBBLEFIELD

COVER JACKET BY
DON COLLINS

SHOAL CREEK PUBLISHERS, INC.
P.O. Box 9737
Austin, Texas 78766

LIBRARY OF CONGRESS CATALOG CARD NO. 75-8061
ISBN NO. 0-88319-021-4

LITHOGRAPHED AND BOUND IN THE UNITED STATES OF AMERICA

DEDICATED TO

ALL ORANGE-BLOODED STUDENTS,

EX-STUDENTS,

FACULTY AND FRIENDS . . .

U.T. AUSTIN TRADITIONS AND NOSTALGIA

Introduction..................................... 13
The Seal.. 15
Hook 'em, 'Horns............................... 18
The University Colors........................... 19
The Alma Mater................................. 23
Texas Fight Song 26
The Santa Rita................................. 27
Bevo... 30
The Tower, the Clock, the Chimes............... 39
Victory Lights 43
Clark Field..................................... 46
Red Candles 50
The Forty Acres 51
The Pansy Bed 52
The Perip....................................... 53
Longhorns 54
Beck's Lake 55
The Battle Oaks 56
St. Peter's Gate 58
Dillingham's Pasture 59
"Smokey" the Cannon 60
Big Bertha...................................... 61
Running The Flag............................... 63
The Old Water Tank........................... 65
The Spirit of Old B. Hall 67
Senior Swing-Out and the Bluebonnet Chain 71
Tea-Sippers 78
Judge Clark Christmas Dinners 79
March 2 Celebration 81
Memorial Stadium 83
U.T. vs. Texas A. & M......................... 86
The Patron Saints.............................. 88
    Alexander Fredericke Clair................... 88
    Peregrinus 90
    Hermes...................................... 92
    Ptah.. 92
Pushball Contest................................ 93
Littlefield Fountain 95

The Mustangs 99
Annual Christmas Carol Program 101
The Daily Texan 102
The Cactus 105
The Blunderbuss 107
Round-Up 110
Scholz's 116
Eeyore's Birthday Party 118
Sunflower Ceremony 120
Commencement 121
The U.T. Senior Ring 124
Austin and the Hill Country 125
Index 127

ILLUSTRATIONS

Aggie Bonfire — 87
Battle Oaks — 56
Becks Lake — 55
B Hall — 67
Bevo — 31
Big Bertha — 61
Campus 1915 — 130-131
Campus 1975 — 2-3
Clair, Alexander Fredericke — 88
Clark Field — 48
Commencement — 123
Dillingham's Pasture — 59
Littlefield Fountain — 96
Longhorns — 54
Hermes — 92
Hook 'Em Horns — 18
March 2nd — 81
Memorial Stadium — 83
Mustangs — 100

Pansy Bed — 52
Peregrinus — 90
Perip — 53
Pushball Contest — 94
Round-Up — 115
Running the Flag — 64
Santa Rita — 29
Scholtz's — 116
Seal — 15
Senior Ring — 124
"Smokey", The Cannon — 60
St. Peters Gate — 58
Tea Sippers — 78
The Texan — 102
Texas Fight Song — 26
The Tower, The Clock,
The Chimes — 38
Victory Lights — 45
Water Tank — 66

PREFACE

This book is intended to be for those who love The University of Texas at Austin and for those who are interested intellectually in what makes a campus unique. The people who have made the University what it is may feel that important omissions have been made. I had great difficulty finding a stopping place; but I've tried, in bold strokes, to produce a sketch all will recognize. One might say that some organizations should be included, because they have had significant roles in developing the traditional activities, but an entire book could be devoted to organizations.

Some readers will find errors of fact; others will find the stories to be different from those they had accepted as truth. Hopefully, these discrepancies will produce interesting conversations when University friends get together and that additional nostalgic stories will be told.

Many people helped me write this book. If I began to enumerate them, I'd be in trouble. I'm grateful to all who helped me find materials, to all who have checked the stories, to all who helped put the manuscript together, and to all who tolerated me while I wrote it.

M. C. B.

June, 1975

INTRODUCTION

Today as traditions are being questioned, scorned and often discarded, perhaps a glimpse into the history of The University of Texas at Austin to identify some of the cultural patterns that have made it unique would be appropriate. Nostalgia tends to dim and even erase memories of unpleasant experiences. Nostalgia selects only what is agreeable and may even distort that or turn it into myth. One writer has suggested that nostalgia is for remembering, while tradition is to be forgotten.

Traditions may be the intangible parts of the campus culture, but they are powerful factors that shape student attitudes and behavior. Traditions determine the artifacts; they also grow up around these artifacts. Each institution has a way of life—a tradition, a set of values, a pattern of customs—that influences and provides a framework for the educational experiences of members of a campus community. Campus culture, like the parent cultures from which it comes, develops and grows, creates new patterns, repeats old ones, and is subject to deliberate modification and change. It is influenced by the culture of the surrounding area, but it develops its own traditions, customs, and ways of life consistent with or opposed to the outside social forces.

We might assume from Ruth Benedict's studies in cultural anthropology that cultures tend to perpetuate themselves and that persons moving into them tend to take on ways of feeling, thinking, and behaving that are in harmony with the culture. Cultural traditions do not die; they live within us and guide us in our future actions. If American student life and customs have changed—and it is obvious that changes have occurred—students today think and act as they do, at least in part, because of their heritage. "What our colleges do," says Nevitt Sanford in the introductory chapter to *The American College*, "tends to be governed by tradition or to be improvised in the face of diverse—usually unanticipated—pressures."

Pervasive traditions that express themselves through a variety of acts and help set the character of a college community are important considerations. Pervasive traditions are difficult to identify but establish norms and relationships that are instrumental in making each college unique.

The selection of some of the traditions at U. T. Austin that have made the culture of the campus what it is must be a continuous selective process. Passage of time causes some traditions to assume greater significance and meaning. Nostalgia, on the other hand, tends to give former students a sense of sophistication; it enables them to feel superior by giving them the opportunity to laugh at simpler times in their lives.

The traditions and traditional activities that follow are proposed as being some of the important ones that shaped the culture of the U.T. Austin campus. Perhaps nostalgia influenced the selection of these in preference to others another would list.

THE SEAL

The University Act of the Legislature of 1881 provided: "The Regents . . . and their successors in office . . . shall have the right of making and using a common seal and of altering the same at pleasure." In accordance with the provision, a committee was appointed at the first meeting of the Board of Regents of The University of Texas, held on November 15, 1881, to design a University seal. Dr. Ashbel Smith, Thomas J. Devine, and Smith Ragsdale were members of the committee which recommended a design that was adopted. The seal was described as follows:

> A Texas star inscribed within a circle, a second circumference being circumscribed leaving a narrow space between the two circumferences, on which shall be engraved the Latin words, *Universitas Texana*, the remaining space, if any, to be filled with some appropriate design, as a vine, or branch with leaves. The space between the parts of the star to be filled with the Latin motto, 'non sine pulvere palma,' was engraved.

Five years passed before twenty-five dollars was appropriated for the purchase of a stamp. Even then, the design embodied in the die was altered. The chief criticism of it was that it was not sufficiently distinctive; it did not embody University colors, and the motto was commonplace. For almost nineteen years, the seal was kept in the background and was rarely seen or seldom used.

Dr. W. J. Battle, Professor of Classical Languages, originated the idea of getting a new seal. In October, 1902, he discussed the idea with President W. L. Prather and then submitted a design drawn under his directions by Charles Young of the firm of Bailey, Banks and Biddle of Philadelphia. Dr. Battle explained the new design as follows:

> In conformity with general usage, the design adopts as its central feature the shield form that shows the origin of heraldic arms. This shield is divided into two fields, the upper white, the lower orange, the University colors. In the lower and larger field are the historic wreath and star of the Great Seal of the State of Texas; in the upper field is the open book, fit symbol of an institution of learning. The shield rests within a circle of blue, the color of sincerity, containing the motto, 'Disciplina Praesidium Civitatis.' This is Professor Edwin W. Fay's terse Latin rendering of the apothegm of President Mirabeau B. Lamar . . . 'Cultivated mind is the guardian genius of democracy.'
>
> Around the disk of blue is a larger disk of red, color of strength, bearing the words *Sigillum Universitatis Texanae*. And addition of the word *Sigillum* is in the interest of clearness, and is, besides, in accord with general use.

President Prather submitted the new seal to the faculty on November 3, 1903, and on their recommendation to the Board of Regents, October 31, 1905, the Regents adopted the new seal. The words, "Seal of The University of Texas," were substituted for the Latin words, "Sigillum Universitatis Texanae."

The new seal rapidly became popular. In 1932, a student reporter told of its popularity:

> The first purchase a freshman makes when he begins his college life probably is a notebook bearing the University seal. He sends his best girl back home a bracelet with the engraved emblem. He can hardly wait for his dad to see his collegiate room with the orange and white pennant hanging on the wall, and the bookends that bear the same stamp. . . . He prepares early for his

first weekend home. His luggage is littered with orange and white stickers and he has an extra supply inside to paste on the windshield of the family car.

In the early spring of 1949, Hulon W. Black, secretary of the Development Board of The University of Texas, asked Dr. Leonardt F. Kreisle, then Assistant Professor of Mechanical Engineering, to prepare a color rendition of the seal. He was asked to work closely with Dr. Battle. Apparently, the 1905 version of the seal had been defined in words only. In May, 1949, Dr. Battle and Dr. Kreisle agreed on a design that was completed in color and presented to the Development Board and to the Board of Regents.

Not until May 4, 1957, did the Regents officially adopt the new rendition. Upon the recommendation of President Logan Wilson and on motion of Mrs. Charles DeVall, seconded by Lee Lockwood, the rendering of the seal by Dr. Kreisle was unanimously adopted by the Regents as the official seal of The University of Texas.

The colors established for the new seal are sometimes indicated by hatching vertical lines for red, horizontal for blue, diagonal across vertical for orange. The seal appears on all official documents and papers of U. T. It is also used on rings, banners, pennants, stationery, T-shirts, and even match-book covers and plastic glasses.

HOOK 'EM, 'HORNS

At the Friday night pep rally in Gregory Gymnasium before the Texas Christian University football game in 1955, the "Hook 'Em, 'Horns" signal was introduced. The signal is made by extending the index and little fingers and by tucking the middle and ring fingers beneath the thumb. The result should resemble the head of a Longhorn.

The sign was introduced by Head Yell Leader, Harley Clark, Jr., now a district judge in Austin. "It came to my attention," he recalled, "that we didn't have a formal sign. A friend (Henry Pitts) and I were just standing around bulling a couple of nights before the pep rally, and it struck me as being a good idea to formally suggest this as our sign."

The idea caught on instantly, and the next day the stands were full of "hook 'em" signs. Today students stand with right arms extended, giving the "Hook 'Em, 'Horns" sign while singing "The Eyes of Texas."

hookum horns
from photo by n.goldforb

THE UNIVERSITY COLORS

"University colors are officially orange and white," *The Ranger,* a weekly campus publication that preceded *The Texan,* proudly announced on April 4, 1900. For several years, the subject had been one that aroused deep feelings and diverse opinions.

In 1885 a group of University students went down to the depot to see the baseball team off for their game with Southwestern University in Georgetown, thirty miles away. One coed had commented that the group of supporters needed some colors. Two young men, one of whom was Venable B. Proctor, ran back up Congress to the nearest store that sold ribbons and asked for two colors—any colors. The two available in quantity were orange and white, and the boys bought six bolts of each color and hurried back to pass out ribbon streamers before the train left.

Edward A. Blount, Jr., related in an article in a 1914 *Alcalde* that in 1891-92 the same colors, orange and white, by a coincidence, were chosen, as at that time there was no "knowledge whatever of the University having any distinctive colors. In fact, very few colleges in the South had even at that time paid any attention to such matters."

Early issues of *The Cactus,* the campus yearbook that was first published in 1894, listed colors as orange and white, but other suggestions were made and disputes arose. A movement was on in 1894 to change the colors to orange and black. The athletic department used orange and maroon. The question as to whether the University would have one color or two was settled in favor of two at a mass meeting, but the students could not agree on what the two would be.

The Board of Regents decided to take a vote of alumni, faculty and students, including those at the

Medical Branch in Galveston. After the vote was taken, the Regents gave final approval to the chosen colors in May, 1900. The final tally showed that of the total vote of 1111, orange and white received 562; orange and maroon, 310; royal blue, 203; royal blue and crimson, 11; crimson, 10; various others, 15. By a majority of thirteen over all other suggestions, orange and white were selected. On a motion of Regent Bryan, the report was received and adopted by the Regents at their meeting on May 10, 1900.

"That is as it should be," a faculty member commented. "Early traditions, unless vicious, should not be trampled upon."

The Regents failed to say what shade of orange would be used. Over the next half century, many shades were used for University uniforms, pennants, publications, and mementos. The shades ranged from near yellow to almost brown, including the dark "burnt orange" in which the athletic department currently clothes its athletes.

Objections to this color inconsistency led to some attempts to select an official shade. When Dr. Leonardt F. Kreisle was concerned with the rendering of the official seal for the Development Board in 1949, he requested the Development Board to provide him with a suitable description of the colors. Hulon Black discussed the description of colors with members of the Board of Regents and reported to Dr. Kreisle that the white was to be a "pure, true white, unblemished with any tone or tint of any color." The orange was defined as a bright orange, similar to that used—at the time—on the ceiling of the exterior entrance foyer of the Texas Union Building. This was a bright orange, of medium to light shade, definitely not a dark, burnt orange. Dr. Kreisle's rendering of the seal as the official Seal of The University of Texas was unanimously adopted by the Board of Regents on May 4, 1957. This rendition of the seal, using a bright orange, has been widely distributed by the Development Board since 1950.

The controversy continued. In 1962, Coach Darrell Royal changed the color of his players' jerseys to a dark burnt orange. He was not the first coach to use the darker shade. In 1928, Coach Clyde Littlefield switched to a dark burnt orange because the jerseys being used at the time had a tendency to fade to a light yellow in hot water. The shade became brighter again during World War II because of a shortage of dye. When local newspapers began publishing stories calling burnt orange the new official color of the University, a number of alumni were outraged. Leading this group was Richard Fleming, a 1915 graduate of the School of Law and founder and developer of the University Writings Collection. Former Orange Jackets and Cowboys remembered the bright orange of their uniforms. Other exes had old bright orange pennants to prove they were correct.

In September, 1966, Fleming and other alumni and students submitted a petition to the Board of Regents protesting the use of burnt orange. On October 6, 1966, Chancellor Harry Ransom appointed a committee to consider the alumni petition concerning the colors and to make recommendations.

After eight months of investigation, the committee presented its recommendation to the Regents on June 17, 1967. The recommendation favored the adoption of burnt orange. The committee report stated that there is little doubt that burnt orange has been used longer than any other hue and that it is widely known as "Texas Orange." At this same Regents' meeting, Fleming and Judge James W. McClendon appeared to oppose the committee's recommendation. The Regents postponed action.

Whether or not a quiet settlement has come about remains to be seen. Athletes still wear burnt orange, a practical shade on the field, but bright orange is still used on many occasions as the real orange that belongs to U. T.

The Eyes of Texas

I once did know a President
  Away down South, in Texas.
And, always, everywhere he went,
  He saw the Eyes of Texas.

The Eyes of Texas are upon you
  All the livelong day,
The Eyes of Texas are upon you,
  You can not get away.
Do not think you can escape them
  At night or early in the morn—
The Eyes of Texas are upon you
  Till Gabriel blows his horn.

Sing me a song of Prexy,
  Of days long since gone by.
Again I seem to greet him
  And hear his kind reply.
Smiles of gracious welcome
  Before my memory rise,
Again I hear him say to me,
  "Remember Texas' Eyes."

John Lang Sinclair

THE ALMA MATER

"Students of The University of Texas, the eyes of Texas are upon you." With these words, William L. Prather often closed his remarks addressed to the student body after he was elected its third president in 1899. Always a figure of perfect dignity and stateliness, he was an alumnus of Washington and Lee University where he had heard President Robert E. Lee say, "The eyes of the South are upon you," and now he paraphrased the remark for Texas students.

J. L. Sinclair, University student in 1903, was the campus poet. Because he was extremely good with the banjo, he had a part in a campus minstrel show given as a benefit for the Varsity track team at the Hancock Opera House on May 12. The night before the show opened, Lewis Johnson, Sinclair's roommate and director of the band, decided the show needed one more peppy song to put it over. The President's words were recalled, and that night John Lang Sinclair composed a song on a piece of wrapping paper torn from a Bosche's laundry bundle. Words were fitted to the tune, "I've Been Working on the Railroad."

His song was a great success when first sung at the minstrel show by the University quartette, whose members were J. R. Cannon, J. D. Kivlehen, Ralph A. Porter, and W. D. Smith. It was introduced in this fashion, Mrs. Mary Lee Prather Darden, daughter of President Prather, related to a student reporter a number of years later:

> During the minstrel a very seedy looking individual appeared wearing an A. & M. sweater and carrying a dilapidated old valise. The interlocutor demanded, "Say, what you got in your bag?"

"A boll weevil. I'se gwine up to the University to show it to the president."

"What for?"

"He's gwine to make a speech to this here boll weevil. He's gwine to tell it, 'The eyes of Texas are upon you.' "

Before the song could be finished, Jim Cannon later recalled, the audience was in an uproar. President Prather was the first to laugh. The audience called for many encores and joined in the singing until the quartette finally had to sing, "We're Tired Out!" Students left the theatre humming and whistling the song. A local daily reported as follows next morning:

> As for Sinclair's song, "The Eyes of Texas Are Upon You," it must be said that the words are taking, that the singing of the quartette . . . was really extraordinary.

The next issue of *The Texan* reported:

> The Varsity quartette next sprung upon the audience that original song, "The Eyes of Texas Are Upon You." How well it was received was attested by the encores that were called for.

The catchy tune immediately became the unofficial alma mater of the University. Until this time, students had used other college songs, but finally Sinclair's song became their own. In 1947, when Sinclair died, "The Eyes of Texas" was played on the Tower carillon at the hour of his funeral.

In 1936, Ed Nunnally, a University student, organized a group to get "The Eyes of Texas" copyrighted. Efforts culminated in the securing of a 28-year copyright of the words and the arrangement. The music itself had long since been in public domain and rightfully belonged to everybody.

The Students' Association owned all rights to the song and collected royalties until January 30, 1964, when the copyright expired. When the time for renewal arrived, the University could not legally ask for a renewal. The author had died, and no heirs could be located. The copyright lapsed, and the song again went into public domain.

An "Eyes of Texas" Committee was formed by the Students' Association after Sinclair's death to begin a scholarship in his memory and to state the copyright policy. Impressive royalties were collected from various users of the song. The John Lang Sinclair Scholarship Fund automatically received half of each royalty received. The greatest sum received was $3,000 from the producers of "Giant" in 1956. Another $1,500 came for the song's use in "The Alamo." Royalties were also paid for the song's use in "Lucy Gallant," "With a Song In My Heart," "Night Train To Galveston," and "Go For Broke."

University President H. Y. Benedict had the song translated into ten foreign languages in 1930.

In 1953, on the fiftieth anniversary of the composition of Sinclair's song, the original text was presented to the Ex-Students' Association on permanent loan by Dr. James L. Johnson and Lewis Johnson. Their father, Lewis Johnson, Sr., had obtained the manuscript from Sinclair. Another copy, a silk-screen, was taken to the moon in 1969 by University ex-student Alan L. Bean. This prized copy is also at the Lila B. Etter Alumni Center on the campus.

TEXAS FIGHT SONG

The original melody for "Texas Taps" was written in 1923 by Walter S. Hunnicutt, who collaborated with James E. King on the Longhorn Band arrangement. Lyrics were composed by Burnett Pharr.

During Texas football games, when the Longhorns score, when they are on a drive, or when things may be going wrong, fans rally to notes of the Texas Fight Song.

Texas Fight! - Texas Fight!
And it's good-bye to A. & M.
Texas Fight! - Texas Fight!
And we'll put over one more win.
Texas Fight! - Texas Fight!
For it's Texas that we love best!
Hail! Hail! The gang's all here,
And it's good-bye to all the rest!

THE SANTA RITA

On June 21, 1916, Dr. John A. Udden, Director of the Bureau of Economic Geology at the University, submitted to the Board of Regents a photograph of a map and a report on the probable or potential mineral resources on the University land in West Texas.

Rupert Ricker was determined to promote the drilling of a wildcat well in Reagan County. Ricker, the son of a Corsicana farmer, attended the University, graduated from Law School in 1915, went to war and then returned home to establish an oil field in Reagan County. Most of Reagan County was University land, and he knew he would have to do business with the University. He rented 431,360 acres from the University for drilling purposes at the rate of ten cents per acre, per year, but he was unable to raise the $43,136 within the allotted thirty days, and he was forced to sell his rights to Frank T. Pickrell and Haymen Krupp of El Paso for $500. Pickrell and Krupp organized Texan Oil and Land Company in April, 1919. They launched a nationwide campaign to solicit investors and commissioned a builder to begin construction of the first derrick before midnight on January 8, 1921, the last day of grace. If no legitimate hole had been drilled by midnight, the permit acquired from the State would expire. Pickrell and his men won the race against time by beginning the hole just before the deadline. This was the original water well, which later dried up. In June of that year, Pickrell employed R. S. McDonald to construct the real oil well derrick. The material was shipped from Ranger for this 84-foot structure.

The name of the well came from a group of Catholic investors in New York, who went to their priest for counsel in the deal. He advised them to invoke the aid of Santa Rita, Saint of the Impossible. They sent a red rose along with their investment to Pickrell, who christened the well Santa Rita, sprinkling the petals of the rose over the derrick and rig structure from the crown block.

Drilling proceeded slowly throughout 1921 and 1922 and into 1923. On Sunday afternoon, May 27, 1923, Carl Cromwell, the driller, and Dee Locklin, the big tool dresser, cleaned out the hole with a bailer at a depth of 3,055 feet and found a little showing of oil. When the bailer was lowered to the bottom of the well again and brought to the surface, it was filled with oil. They decided to tell no one, built a trap door close to the hole, and boarded up the bottom of the derrick.

On Monday morning, May 28, 1923, Mrs. Cromwell heard a hissing noise as she was preparing breakfast. The noise sounded like the hiss of a rattlesnake. She alerted her husband and little daughter, and as they looked out of their door, they saw a column of gas and oil vapor spouting from the top of the well.

"Well, I'll be damned!" Cromwell exclaimed. Pickrell, then in Arkansas, was summoned back and upon reaching the Santa Rita, he found he had a flowing well in the center of sixty-four square miles of leases.

The Santa Rita No. 1 flowed three times on that day, two times on May 29, and once regularly every day thereafter for thirty-five to forty days. At first, production averaged 100 barrels per day; and as soon as pumping operations began, it increased to 200 barrels per day.

The Santa Rita strike began a trend in oil mining on University lands that by 1970 had produced income exceeding $550 million—divided two-thirds to U.T. and one-third to Texas A. & M. The 1876 *Constitution* provided that proceeds from the sale of any portion of the lands should become a Permanent Fund, a University endowment. Later, legal interpretations provided that oil was a part of the landed endowment. The Available Fund or interest from the Permanent Fund, could be used as the Regents of the two schools directed. Litigation slowed immediate use of the new wealth, but within ten years from the discovery event, the University started a major building program.

The original Santa Rita rig stayed on its location for nineteen years, intermittently pumping oil. In 1939, University history professor Dr. Walter Prescott Webb recommended that the rig be moved to the campus to serve as "a symbol of the great era in the history of the University." It was dismantled in January, 1940, and shipped to Austin, but no site was selected for it and it was put in storage for 18 years.

Leroy Jeffers, then chairman of the Board of Regents, presented a plan to erect Santa Rita at its present site under the auspices of the Texas State Historical Association. On a cool, rainy Thanksgiving Day, November 27, 1958, Texas and A. & M. were preparing for a nationally televised football game at Memorial Stadium in Austin. Just before kickoff, they took time out to memorialize Santa Rita, the Saint of the Impossible, who brought both schools great riches.

The old rig now stands on the corner of Trinity and Nineteenth Street as a monument to probably the biggest surge of change in the University's history.

BEVO

". . . in the scientific history of its development, the Longhorn comes to connote courage, fighting ability, nerve, lust of combat, efficiency in deadly encounters, and the holy spirit of never-say-die."

The Alcalde, March, 1920

Brought to the New World by the Spaniards in their early settlement of the Southwest, the Longhorn breed gradually evolved. The animals developed long horns to fend off enemies. Those with the longest horns survived. As the breed was becoming extinct by the early part of the twentieth century, private groups and state agencies began efforts to preserve the Longhorns.

Varsity teams had been referred to as Longhorns since 1904, but if anyone had considered acquiring a live Longhorn steer as a University mascot before Thanksgiving, 1916, plans did not materialize.

Bevo I

Stephen Pinckney (1911) spearheaded a movement to provide a live mascot for The University of Texas. He collected $1.00 each from 124 alumni and purchased a Longhorn steer that was located "somewhere in the Texas Panhandle." The steer was shipped to Austin, without food or water, in a boxcar. By the time he arrived, he was aptly described by a *Texan* reporter as "the most recalcitrant freshman ever bulldozed into higher education." He had horns measuring seven or eight feet from tip to tip.

On Thanksgiving Day of 1916, the frightened steer was dragged onto the field by two lusty cowboys and formally presented to the students in a short speech (audible only to the student section) by T. B. Buffington of the class of 1892.

I have been requested to present to The University of Texas a mascot or protecting spirit that now and in future years will bring good luck to the institution and its teaching. Behold him! The Longhorn of Texas, emblematic as he stands of the fighting spirit of progress as well as of the more modest angel of use. He conquered the wide prairies and the forests. . . . In spite of tick and vile mosquito, he made a restful bed among the soft mosses and nodding flowers. He fought with the sullen fevers of southern climes and breasted with stern patience the wild blizzards of the North. Yet, withal, he fed the hungry millions, and many a dainty foot with him has walked in beauty and in safety down the roughened road of life.

As the great longhorn was free to roam the wilderness of Texas, so must the University be free to roam the world of thought, unhampered and unafraid.

Upon the present occasion this old Longhorn, luckgiver, is doubly welcome in our midst. The times are propitious. Let him do his work and give victory to eleven smaller, but as valiant and aggressive, Longhorns who battle this day for the glory of our halls.

In order that he may make no mistake, I will speak to him in his own language:

> Now old cow, we have put you where
> You can do some good with your horns and hair.
> Take off that dignity, rub off that frown;
> Put on a sweater, not a cap and gown.

> Get in the game as a mascot should
> And show these bullies that you can make good.
> And after the game with a victory won,
> We will toot 'em up, you old son of a gun!

Beloved University, I present to you this Longhorn steer.

The score of that Thanksgiving Day game was 21-7 in favor of Texas over Texas A. & M. This score was sweet revenge for the 13-0 defeat by A. & M. in 1915, the first time the two teams had played since 1911 because of a post-game brawl.

In celebration of the 1916 victory, a *Texan* reporter announced that a large "T" and the "21-7" score would be branded on the side of the new mascot. Under student protests of cruelty, the branding was not performed but the idea apparently provided inspiration for spiteful Aggies. The steer had an enormous appetite, and feeding him became a problem. By February 1917, he had been moved, by action of the Students' Assembly, from a ranch several miles out of town to some southside stockyards where he could be fed for 60c per day. The Athletic Council disclaimed him, saying he was presented to the entire student body.

On Sunday morning, February 11, as J. W. Searight, owner of the South Austin stockyards, made his rounds, he found that the mascot had been branded with eight-inch numbers, "13-0," score of the A. & M. dominated game of 1915. A news story of the treacherous event was on the back page of the next issue of The Daily Texan, but the editor wrote in his column:

> . . . Regardless of who branded the Longhorn steer "13-0," it is done. We might confess that the joke is on us, and the only way to maintain our record for clean sportsmanship is to wait for time to even things up down at College Station next season. We hope that the steer recovers from the eight-inch imprint, reminding us of that uneventful Friday, and only wish that much of our talk of public branding had been put into actual practice.
>
> Since the animal costs the student body of the University $18 per month to feed, and since he no longer resembles a specimen of which we could justly be proud, why should not the Assembly order him shipped c.o.d. to College Station, with a price of 21 plus 7 or $28 attached? This seems the only logical procedure, unless we butcher the brute.

Not about to confess the joke, a group of U. T. students conceived a scheme to save face. They altered the numerals "13-0" to read "BEVO" by simply changing the "13" to a "B," the "-" to "E," and inserting "V" before "0." "Bevo" just happened to be the brand of a popular near beer, product of the Budweiser Company during this period of prohibition.

In March of that year, Bevo was grazing free of charge, on a 20,000 acre ranch located sixteen miles from Austin. He was guarded by policemen when rumors prevailed that the Aggies planned to capture him.

Bevo remained on grazing land until he was brought into Austin in 1920 for his final appearance. On January 20, he was served as barbecue to over one hundred guests, principally T-men and coeds who had won letters in women's athletics. Steve Pinckney was present; and a delegation from A. & M. was on hand for the banquet and to receive the half of Bevo's hide that had been branded. His head and horns were mounted and hung in the U. T. athletic office.

Bevo II

The successor to the first Bevo came from the 10,000 acre Diamond-T ranch 430 miles from Austin. W. A. Boyett, father of Lynwood Boyett, former head yell leader, and Jack Boyett, yell leader in 1932, presented Bevo II to The University of Texas students as the surprise feature of a "surprise" rally of 4,200 on the night before the Texas-S.M.U. football game in the fall of 1932. The students roared with delight when the big Longhorn was dragged in front of Gregory Gymnasium. Lynn Boyett made the presentation speech, and John McCurdy of the Ex-Students' Association accepted the mascot. McCurdy said, "The Longhorn steer as an animal type is passing away, but the spirit of which that type is symbolic is not passing away!"

In the game the next day, Bevo II did not respond graciously to the cordial reception he received from the crowd. He kicked at the side boards of the trailer in which he was riding and tried to break the trailer gate. An S.M.U. yell leader gave him a cudgelling with a megaphone, and the rambunctious steer had to be removed from the field. His only other public appearances were at the head of the parade before the T.C.U. game and in the stadium at the A. & M. game. Kindhearted students tried to overlook "his cagey disposition and his refusal to conform to standards of campus behavior," and kept up their donations of oats and hay. His four-feet span of horns and his 500 pounds of beef grew faster than did the Longhorn offensive.

By Christmas, it was back to the range for Bevo II. The Athletic Council ruled 5 to 1 that he was not to enter the stadium again, but the expense of his upkeep was the deciding factor in sending him back to the Diamond-T.

Bevo III

At a pep rally on Friday, November 16, 1945, preceding the T.C.U. game, Bevo III made his first appearance. He was a "rip-snorting, fence-busting steer," an appropriate mascot for the post-war campus. He was about two years old when he was placed in the custody of the Silver Spurs, honorary service organization, by Charles Schreiner, a member. (Schreiner is now owner of the Y O ranch at Mountain Home.) Schreiner also conducted a campus drive to outfit the Spurs in new uniforms and to provide a trailer for Bevo. Bevo III was kept for three years and was then sent into retirement to the San Antonio Zoo.

Bevo IV

Considered to be the "meanest of them all," Bevo IV was acquired in the fall of 1949. A student reporter described him in *The Daily Texan*:

> Just about the biggest, wildest, rarin'-est steer you've ever seen. Two thousand pounds of beef, stretched over a frame that measures approximately 19 hands high, with a horn spread of four feet and horns that stand three feet high . . . that's Bevo.

Bevo IV was eight years old when he was acquired from the Texas State Parks Board and was never trained for his role as mascot. He was kept for only one year.

Bevo V

The next Bevo, acquired in 1950, was only one and one-half years old. History relegates him to a mediocre position among the animals that have served as mascots, but he was tame and served for five years. He escaped the ill treatment of some former Bevos at the O. U. games in Dallas. The Sooners had managed to saw off horns of some former mascots, but heavy guard at the 1950 game prevented the act on Bevo V.

Bevo VI

Acquired in 1955 from Ft. Griffin State Park near Albany, the two-year-old Bevo VI apparently could not endure the screaming and confusion of football games, because he once broke loose and ran over the Rice bench at half-time. As he was a potential trouble-maker, he was kept only two seasons.

Bevo VII

Bevo VII, the most beloved of the U. T. Longhorns, had been on loan from the State Parks Board, which maintains a herd of the famed steers. He was acquired in 1957 when he was only four months old and was kept as a mascot for eight years. Known as a gentle steer, he loved crowds and relished attention.

His illustrious history included celebration of a national football championship in 1963. In November of 1963, he was kidnapped by students from Texas A. & M. but was in good condition when recovered. The incident stirred statewide interest. The Spurs collected $3,000 for his air fare to the Orange Bowl game in 1965.

Old age and arthritis caught up with Bevo in 1965, however, and he was no longer able to make out-of-town trips. He was finally put out to pasture.

Bevo VIII

Major S. R. Parten of Houston, former member of the University Board of Regents, sold Bevo VIII to the Silver Spurs for $1.00. They resold him to the State for the same amount in order that he could be boarded at the State Hog Farm. Major Parten was recognized and

Bevo VIII was officially presented in his first appearance at Memorial Stadium on October 23, 1965, in a pre-game announcement.

Bevo VIII, known as "Old Will," was actually acquired as a temporary mascot, because he was too old to be trained and was usually restless at games. His horns were slightly longer than those of his predecessors, but he was not a member of the bloodline of former Bevos.

Bevo VIII's reign was for only one year, after which he, too, was turned out to pasture. He was retired on September 17, 1966.

Bevo IX

Born in February, 1966, Bevo IX, an orange and white animal, was selected during the following summer to be the new mascot. He came from Fort Griffin State Park and is property of the State of Texas.

Bevo IX was officially presented as a mascot at half-time of the football game with Southern California in Memorial Stadium on September 17, 1966. He was sired by a bull named Sampson from the Schreiner's Y O ranch. He was usually well-behaved at games, but his unusual characteristic was that he didn't like women. He was kept, during his tenure, at the State Health Department farm with two of his predecessors, the feeble Bevo VII and Old Will, Bevo VIII.

Old age forced Bevo IX out to pasture. He was retired at the end of the 1975 football season. He weighed between 1,300 and 1,400 pounds, and his horns measured 48 inches from tip to tip.

Bevo X

Born of registered stock on March 23, 1972, on the Hardin ranch near Vernon, Bevo X began his reign on September 18, 1976 at the first home football game. He is on loan to the University from John Hardin III, a member of the Silver Spurs. He weighs more than 1,000 pounds and has a hornspan of 43 inches.

THE TOWER,
THE CLOCK, THE CHIMES

The Tower of the Main Building, completed in 1937, stands as an identity symbol for The University of Texas at Austin. Until the mid-1960s, the Tower and the Capitol were the two structures that stood out in the Austin skyline. As other tall buildings began to appear, some citizens began to complain that these two important structures were losing their identity.

The Main Building, with its Tower, was designed by Paul P. Cret of Philadelphia. The stone is Bedford Indiana limestone and the style is modified Spanish Renaissance. Crowned by what is sometimes called the Greek outhouse, the Tower rises boldly above everything. It is 59 feet square and 307 feet tall. (The State Capitol is 311 feet. Visitors are often told that the Capitol sits on an elevation 600 feet above sea level and the Tower site is 606 feet. By these devious calculations, the Tower enjoys a two foot advantage.)

Above the twenty-seventh floor is the observation deck. Above the deck, and set back several feet, rises the portion of the Tower that supports four faces of a huge clock, the diameter of which is more than twelve feet. The clock marks the quarter-hour by four bells of the Westminster Chime and strikes the hours on a bell that weighs three and a half tons. The bells—seventeen in all—hang in the square colonnaded belfrey that rests on the clock-story and forms the crowning feature of the Tower. A complete carillon has 35 bells, but the one at U. T. is incomplete in that it has only 17.

The bells, which weigh 40,000 pounds, were cast by the Old Meneely Bell Foundry of Watervliet, New York, and were installed in the Tower in 1936. They are made of "bell metal," 78 percent copper and 22 percent tin. The hammers are iron and, like the bells, are covered with bronze. A study committee, composed of Lutcher Stark, chairman of the Board of Regents; Dr. W. J. Battle, chairman of the building committee; Mrs. I. D. Fairchild, member of the Board of Regents; and R. L. White, supervising architect of the University, made an attempt to listen to chimes in different parts of the country. The type selected was similar to the bells at Valley Forge. In the early years—until 1968—the carillonneur played on a mechanical keyboard, a clavier, located in the bell tower that was open to the sky. His only protection was a hut built around the keyboard. Today the "chime room" is a small room, scarcely larger than a walk-in-closet, on the third floor of the Main Building. The area is bare of all furniture except a keyboard that resembles a small electric organ. The carillonneur sits on a wooden bench. The small room has its own thermostat and is comfortable in any weather. An amplifier to the left of the keyboard enables the carillonneur to hear what he is playing without a time lag. A pipe along the wall is filled with wires and when a player presses a key, the wires relay an electrical impulse to a clapper inside a bell.

Janet Yantis, a high school student and the daughter of U.T. construction inspector H. C. Yantis, was the first to play the carillon. The first tune was, appropriately, "The Eyes of Texas." The first concert was played on the carillon by Dr. Paul Boner as President H. Y. Benedict lay in state in the gymnasium on the campus.

To the poetically-minded, the chimes say:

Lord, through this hour
Be Thou my guide,
For in Thy power
I do confide.

In 1938, when the College of Fine Arts was established, weekly carillon concerts were given. These gradually increased to three times weekly. The carillonneur plays a ten minute concert each day at 12:50 p.m. The chimes are also played at Commencement and on other special occasions. Among the students and staff members who have served as carillonneur are Eldon Sutton, Proctor Crow, Paul Moore, James Moeser, Lee Rigsby, Marion Carnes, Jim Owen, David Anderson, Charles Carlton, and Tom Anderson, the current one.

The big clock, which serves as the principal time piece for the campus community, was first set in running order when it arrived in 1936 by J. R. (Uncle John) Blocker. It was cleaned and polished in 1948 and again in 1968. Events on the Tower have attracted statewide and nationwide attention. A fire in August, 1965, on the twentieth floor damaged part of the Hoblitzelle Theatre Arts Library. Sparks from an acetylene torch apparently set fire to some books. Heavy fire and water damage resulted on the twentieth floor and heat and smoke damage occurred on the nineteenth and twenty-first floors.

The Tower has been the site of nine deaths, seven of which were suicides. The most tragic event associated with the structure, however, occurred at noon on August 1, 1966, when Charles Joseph Whitman, a 25-year-old student of architectural engineering, turned the Tower into his fortress. Armed with three rifles, 700 rounds of ammunition, and other weapons, he terrorized unsuspecting persons on the campus and in the University community. Sixteen were killed and 32 others were wounded. Whitman's wife and mother were his first victims. He had killed them early that same morning to spare them the embarrassment of his actions. Ninety minutes after the shooting began, four police officers and one civilian reached Whitman on the Tower. Officer Rumiro Martinez, at the time, was alleged to have killed Whitman with a shotgun blast. Classes were dismissed the following day, and flags flew at half-mast. The Tower remained closed for several weeks. One note left by Whitman requested an autopsy to determine if he suffered from mental illness. The autopsy revealed a brain tumor, which had caused Whitman to suffer severe headaches.

After a young man jumped from the Tower on October 28, 1974, the observation deck was again closed until some form of protective barrier could be designed and erected.

J. Frank Dobie suggested that the Tower be laid on its side so that all rooms would be close to the ground with a "gallery running around the front of it." He remarked to his class in Southwestern literature while the Tower was being built, "It's the most ridiculous thing I ever saw. With as much room as there is in Texas and as many acres of land as the University owns, we have to put up a building like those in New York."

Through the years, the Tower has become a symbol with different meanings to different people. It has been one of the area's biggest tourist attractions because of the view. It stands as a symbol of victory or defeat after athletic contests. To numerous alumni all over the world, it has a significance that is personal to each one. It symbolizes the University.

VICTORY LIGHTS

When the Tower was constructed, a spectacular system for floodlighting it was installed. The system consisted of ninety-six units of 750 and 1,000 watts capacity on the tenth floor and of sixty-four 250 watt units on the observation deck. On the first offset below the column deck were forty-eight 500 watt units, and on the top parapet wall were eighty-four 100 watt units. The floodlights were remote-controlled from small push button switches on the main switchboard in the basement.

The history of the orange lights dates back to 1937, when they were first tested. This happened during football season and officials thought it might be appropriate to clothe the Tower in orange when the Longhorns won.

Just when to use the orange lights became a controversial issue. In October, 1947, a committee of seven met with Carl J. Eckhardt, Superintendent of University Utilities, and officially decided the "burning" issue. A few revisions have been made since that date so that today the schedule for the Victory Lights is as follows:

I. *Complete Tower Orange:*
    1. On nights of National Collegiate Athletics Association or Association for Intercollegiate Athletics for Women national team championships or ties in any sport. In case of ties, alternate sides of the column deck will be orange and white.
    2. On nights of football victories over Texas A&M University and Sunday night following such victories only.

43

II. *Tower Shaft White, Observation and Column Decks Orange:*
1. On nights of football victories or ties other than those involving Texas A&M.
2. On nights on which a Southwest Conference or Texas Association for Intercollegiate Athletics for Women championship or tie is won in any team sport.
3. On nights of each victory in NCAA or AIAW team District or regional championships so long as the team is in the running for the national championship.
4. Annual Commencement, Honors Day and upon the occasion of the inaugural of the President of The University of Texas at Austin.
5. On March 2, April 21, Easter, Memorial Day (the last Monday in May), July 4 and December 25.

Victory Lights will not be displayed for any scheduled victory on a night other than the one upon which the victory occurs with but one exception: the Sunday night following a football victory over Texas A&M.

In 1973, the regularly used white Tower lights were turned off as a reminder to the University and Austin communities of the need to conserve energy. Student leaders were among the first to recommend this move. William M. Wilcox, director of the University's physical plant, described the energy load required to light the Tower as "negligible" with the primary purpose for turning off the lights as "psychological." A decision was made by the University's Energy Conservation Committee, however, to retain the tradition of the orange victory Tower. The committee noted that adherence to the established schedule for victory lights would mean Tower lights would be turned on a maximum of 15 to 20 nights during the year. It announced that lighting the sky with an orange Tower on those nights would serve as a reminder of the 345 nights each year that the Tower no longer shines. In the fall of 1974, however, the Tower was again lighted in accordance with its regular schedule.

On October 11, 1977, on order of President Lorene Rogers, the Tower was completely orange to honor Dr. Ilya Prigogine, winner of the 1977 Nobel Prize in chemistry.

CLARK FIELD

In 1887, an athletic field was constructed where Taylor Hall now stands. There were no grandstands or bleachers, and fans stood around the field or sat in their buggies and tally-hos and watched the games. The field was used by both the baseball and football teams during these early years.

In 1899, the owner, a Mr. de Cordova, demanded his land. The athletic department contracted to buy it for $3,000—$1,000 down and $1,000 for the next two years. In the third year, the department was in debt and could not make its payment. The student body voluntarily pledged $1,460 worth of library deposits, and the ugly vacant lot became the University's official athletic field.

In 1904, *Texan* editors D. A. Frank and John Townes led a drive to name the field for Judge James Benjamin Clark, who had served as Proctor for U. T. since 1883. As Proctor, he performed duties as manager of buildings and grounds, dean of students, registrar, business manager, admissions officer, and secretary to the faculty.

Clark Field changed as athletics grew in popularity and as attendance at games increased. In the early days, spectators stood around the sidelines or sat in horse-drawn carriages. Later, a few bleachers were built on one side. After the Texas team played football at the University of Missouri in the fall of 1907 and saw new bleachers on that campus that students themselves had built, they returned home and sparked a campaign to build bleachers before the game with A. & M. ten days later. The editor of *The Texan* wrote of the need for new bleachers and said it was ". . . unbecoming in a school of the standing and size of Texas to tolerate this inadequacy longer." A rousing rally was held and a huge banner, made by girls in the Woman's Building, was auctioned to the highest bidder. The Engineers paid $325 for the banner and began a fund for the bleachers. Student volunteer carpenters arranged to be excused from classes, and the bleachers were completed before the big game. In 1911, the Athletic Council decided to construct a covered grandstand. Students were again asked to do the construction work, but the idea was not their own and enthusiasm was lacking. By 1916 Clark Field was in better condition to accommodate increasing numbers of spectators. One former student wrote of her impressions:

> Really, none of you would recognize the athletic field—so civilized it has become! It was in the form of a hollow square with grandstands on four sides, and these were simply jammed and packed with enthusiastic humanity—the crowd, I believe, was estimated at between 12,000 and 15,000—rooting, too, has developed into a fine art. . . .

The failures of the past on the athletic field were to change with the arrival of Uncle Billy Disch in 1911. In 1913, Disch's Longhorns easily won the Southwest Conference baseball championship, beginning a streak of fifteen championships that lasted until the old Clark Field was closed at the end of the 1927 season.

The Longhorn football team moved into Memorial Stadium in 1924, and the baseball team finally moved after the 1927 season when the engineering department claimed old Clark Field as the future location of Taylor Hall. Once at the new field (at the corner of Red River and 23rd Streets), the winning tradition of Longhorn baseball continued.

"Billy Goat Hill," a limestone ledge towering from 12 to 15 feet in the outfield of the ball park, actually worked to the Longhorn's advantage during the early years. Texas players were used to it, but visiting opponents spent embarrassing moments sliding down while trying to catch a ball. The new Clark Field, "Billy Goat Hill" and all, was dedicated at the opening game in the 1928 season, when the 'Horns played the Detroit Tigers. Texas lost 12-8, but the trend did not continue after conference play began. Texas again won the Conference.

Uncle Billy Disch retired in 1941, and Bibb Falk, a former star at Texas, became coach. He matched the prolific winning capabilities of Disch in a distinguished career. When he retired in 1967, Cliff Gustafson became coach.

Clark Field's foul lines measured 313 feet to the left, 341 feet to the center, and 300 feet to the right. Balls hit into left field had to travel 350 feet to clear the fence; to clear the fence in center field, they had to

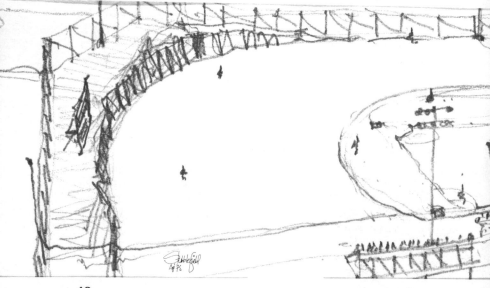

travel 401 feet. The infield was originally seeded with Bermuda grass. The tall rustic wooden fences and the manual scoreboard atop "Billy Goat Hill" gave the park a picturesque look.

On April 3, 1929, 5,000 spectators watched the New York Yankees defeat Texas 8-6. Lou Gehrig was one of the players.

On September 11, 1972, the Regents decided to move the baseball field again. This time it would be located on a six-acre tract of U. T. Austin property east of Interstate Highway 35, at the corner of East 19th and Comal. On September 14, 1973, the Regents awarded a contract of $1,966,747 for constructing the new Clark Field. The total project cost approximately $2,500,000. It has a covered stadium of 5,000 seats, dressing facilities, concession areas, and a lighted artificially surfaced playing field designed for multipurpose activities. The new field, opened officially for the 1975 season, has been named Disch-Falk Field, honoring Uncle Billy Disch and Bibb Falk.

RED CANDLES

The red candle tradition began in November, 1941, when the Longhorns were scheduled to play the Aggies at College Station. Texas had not defeated Texas A. & M. on Kyle Field turf since 1923, and the outcome seemed glum as the undefeated Aggies were heading for the Rose Bowl.

Two stories are told about the beginning of the tradition. One is that on Tuesday before this Thanksgiving Day game, some Alpha Phi's started a candle at their house with the intention of keeping it lighted until the Longhorns left for College Station, where they would defy the 18-year-old hex. On Wednesday morning the girls at the Zeta Tau Alpha house literally built a fire under their spirit and detailed a "watch" to see that the candle kept burning.

The other story is that worried University students visited Madame Augusta Hipple, a local fortune teller, who recommended burning red candles during the week as a sure way to put the hex on A. & M. Her instructions were followed carefully and the move was successful. The Longhorns won with a smashing score of 23 to 0. This method of defying the hex worked from 1941 until 1955 when the Texas red candles were snuffed out by T. C. U. in Memorial Stadium.

Several examples of use of the candles are often cited. In 1950, S. M. U. was number one in the nation with Fred Benners and Kyle Rote as stars; the Longhorns were number seven. Texas beat S. M. U., 23-20. In 1953, the vicious Baylor Bears, third in the nation, rolled into Austin in the smoke of the red candles and were defeated 21-20.

Red candles are still burned occasionally before games.

50

THE FORTY ACRES

The elevated terrain in Austin on which the University is located embraced only forty acres of land at one time. This site was selected when the City of Austin was surveyed for the state capital and was for many years called "College Hill."

Many beautiful live oaks and other kinds of trees on the hill were cut down during the Civil War by order of General John B. Magruder in order to place cannons there to defend the City of Austin.

Boundaries of the Forty Acres were Guadalupe Street on the west from Twenty-First to Twenty-Fourth Streets; along Twenty-Fourth Street to Speedway on the north; Speedway on the east from Twenty-Fourth to Twenty-First Street; and Twenty-First Street on the south from Speedway to Guadalupe.

The Forty Acres, with the exception of Clark Field acquired in 1899 and located just east of the campus, remained the sole block of land making up the campus until approximately four hundred fifty acres along the Colorado River between the city and the Austin dam were given to the University by Colonel George W. Brackenridge of San Antonio on June 17, 1910. After a spirited drive, supported by President Robert E. Vinson and the Regents, to move the campus to the Brackenridge land on the river, the Thirty-Seventh Legislature appropriated, in 1921, the sum of $1,350,000 for the purchase of 135 acres of land north and east of the University as an addition to the original campus.

Since that time, the original Forty Acres has become approximately 400 acres of land, not counting the Brackenridge tract or other holdings away from the main campus.

THE PANSY BED

Through the years—since the mid-thirties when a big round flower bed was built in the center of the walk on the West Mall—pansies have been regularly planted each fall and have bloomed until May, when the summer sun becomes too warm.

During the first week in September, the pansy seeds are usually planted in a greenhouse under the supervision of the landscape gardener. By Thanksgiving, they are ready to be transplanted in the bed on the Mall. Students, faculty and visitors enjoy the blooms all winter and spring and have often chosen the pansy bed as a meeting site.

After the pansies are removed from the bed, a hardier shrub is planted for the summer.

THE PERIP

"Let's make the Perip," a phrase once popular on the campus, has lost the glamour it held for students in the early 1900s. Major George Littlefield gave $3,000 to the University in the spring of 1901 to build a Peripatus, or walk, around the Forty Acres that had been marked by a fence. As $3,000 was not sufficient to build the walk, a professor started the movement to complete the job. The movement was successful and the Peripatus was built.

From the beginning, it was popular with students. The Perip was the ideal place for campus dates, for a walk after dinner, or for meeting friends. Promenade concerts by the University Band on Saturday nights in the spring were quite popular.

The businessmen of Austin raised money in the spring of 1913 to pave the Perip. The new walk made a hike around the campus more pleasant, especially after a heavy rain.

As the campus expanded and additional walks were built, the Perip lost its identity to students and faculty, but one can—if he tries—still take a walk on the Perip.

LONGHORNS

For years, the University football team was unofficially called "varsity" or "Steers." It was not referred to as "Longhorns" until fall, 1904.

In that year, Texas competed in football, baseball, and track, as well as in debate and oratory. Contests took place in twelve states and the Indian Territory. A director of outdoor athletics was hired that year because the Regents, "recognizing the great possibilities for good and the dangers of evil in college athletics, decided to abolish the plan of having temporary and often even irresponsible coaches secured by the students themselves to train the teams."

The term "Longhorns" was still not used consistently as the name for the teams. In 1913, however, H. J. Lutcher Stark, one of the University's greatest benefactors, made his annual donation of warm-up blankets to the football team, and the word "Longhorns" was sewn on each blanket. Sports writers and students liked the name and it was made official. Three years later, a Longhorn steer became the mascot.

In more recent years, the term " 'Horns" is often used to refer to University teams.

BECK'S LAKE

Beck's Lake, or pond, a shallow puddle about three feet wide along the graveled walk at the northwest side of the Library (now Battle Hall), was created by the Superintendent of Grounds, Harry Birk Beck, for whom it was named. He piped in enough water to fall over the old stones left from construction of the Old Main building, planted some willow trees, and placed a bench nearby. The "lake" was only three or four feet in diameter.

Crude as it was, Beck's Lake served as a lovers' rendezvous for a number of years. It was also the scene of many ducking parties. Some students claimed that the water in the lake came from bath tubs in the Woman's Building, not far away, but the source of the water did not lessen the popularity of the trysting place.

Beck's Lake gave way to progress, when, in 1932, a tunnel was constructed from the Power Building to the new Architecture Building.

THE BATTLE OAKS

A legend relating to three old trees, "the Battle Oaks," that still stand on the northwest corner of the campus, became a part of campus tradition. A student reporter told the story in *The Daily Texan:*

Even before the time of the white man, the trees grew. The legend is told of how the largest of the trees listened to the Indian tongue, loved it and learned it. Later the tree brought happiness to an Indian brave by whispering to him of the maiden who loved him, for beneath the branches of the tree she had cried out her love for the warrior. Together they visited the oaks and were perhaps the first Americans and Texans to love them.

When the white man came, the oaks learned the ways of the new race and in times of trouble the white settlers sought comfort beneath their branches. It is related that the oaks brought solace to an old man whose only son had been killed in war.

With the Civil War came the Northern troops. When word was received that they were in Galveston, the hill of oaks was destroyed so that a fortress might be erected to protect the Capitol, with General Magruder in command. All the oaks except the well-known three were sacrificed.

The University grew and the oaks became a favorite spot of the students. In the early days of the Institution, when men and women students were not allowed the freedom they now enjoy, the oaks served as a favorite meeting place.

When plans were being made to build the Biology building, the three oaks were again endangered. This time Dr. J. W. Battle took a determined position to save the trees—and did. As the late J. W. Calhoun reported in a small unpublished manuscript, "Trees on the Campus of the University," the controversy began about 1923. Over the years, the story has been richly embellished to include a not-so-factual but interesting tale of how Dr. Battle sat with a shotgun under the trees and defied the administration axe. Whatever happened, the Biology building was located farther east and the trees were saved.

These same trees now often provide shade for a Round-Up barbeque, for a rock concert, or for a lazy afternoon with a book.

ST. PETER'S GATE

The Twenties were characterized by an increase in automobiles on the campus. During the 1925-26 school year, all roads leading to the campus except the one on the south at the end of University Avenue were blocked. B. B. Neans, the "campus cop," became the guardian to the entrance to the campus, and at Christmas, a little house was built to protect him from cold and rain.

Mr. Nean's little house was moved to the north side of the campus, at Twenty-Fourth and Whitis, before school opened in September, 1932. There Mr. Neans, or St. Pete, as he was called, stood at the campus gate to keep students from driving on the campus during classes.

As the years passed and the University security force increased, one of its duties was to direct traffic into the campus. In the late 1960s, the name was changed to University Police. Five entrances to the campus are now marked by attractive, air-conditioned buildings, constructed in the mid-1960s.

Old-timers still call the 24th and Whitis entrance "St. Peter's Gate," and students still say it's just about as difficult to enter.

DILLINGHAM'S PASTURE

In the 1930s, "Navajo parties" were popular. "Take a Navajo [blanket], an alarm clock and your best girl, rent a Ford and start out," a student wrote.

Farmer H. N. Dillingham's pasture, eight miles out on the Georgetown turnpike, was the best known place to park. For twenty-five cents, students had the privilege of parking undisturbed; and about thirty minutes before dormitories would close (at 11:00 during the week and at 12:00 on week-ends), Mr. Dillingham began ringing his big bell to warn students that it was time to go back to the campus. He would even get on his old dark bay horse and, accompanied by three black dogs, would ride from car to car as closing time approached.

This "supervised parking" on Mr. Dillingham's 100-acre sheep farm provided security from thieves, vandals and lesser rogues.

"SMOKEY" THE CANNON

Operated by the Texas Cowboys, a service organization, little Smokey is a cannon that is fired when Texas makes a score—or an unusually good play—at football games.

"Smokey" was built in U. T.'s mechanical engineering laboratory in 1953 as an answer to the shotgun blasts fired by an Oklahoma University group called the Rufnecks. It was at first actually an aerial cannon that delivered its second and loudest blast 100 feet in the air.

Twice "Smokey" has survived the threats to its use. At the end of the 1954 Thanksgiving game, a hastily-fired shot close to the stands exploded inside the barrel. This shot brought complaints from a woman who said she suffered temporary deafness and received a burnt hole in her dress. The cannon was modified to accommodate a double-barrel 10-gauge shot gun for the 1955 season. Eventually it was changed to shoot 12-gauge blanks.

Before the 1966 season, the Southwest Conference faculty representatives outlawed all cannons for conference games because of the growing danger, but "Smokey" continued in use for nonconference games. The SWC embargo on the use of cannons was lifted after the 1969 season.

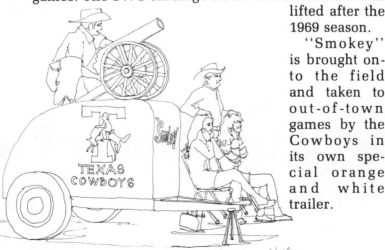

"Smokey" is brought onto the field and taken to out-of-town games by the Cowboys in its own special orange and white trailer.

BIG BERTHA

"Big Bertha," reportedly the world's largest drum, became a fixture of the Longhorn Band during the 1955 football season. Presented to the Band by Colonel D. Harold Byrd of Dallas, the drum is eight feet in diameter, 44 inches in width, stands 10 feet tall on her four-wheel cart, and weighs about 500 pounds. Five "drum wrangler" bandsmen attend her.

"Big Bertha" is more than a big drum; she is also a symbol of the bigness of the Longhorn Band, known as the "Show Band of the Southwest."

"Big Bertha" was originally constructed for the University of Chicago in 1922. Then a member of the Big Ten football conference, Chicago commissioned the Conn Music Company to build the big drum to help create team spirit. The Swift Packing Company kept its biggest cowhides for a year, and the drum was made to fit those hides. Chicago abandoned football, and Bertha lay silent under the stadium.

During the following few years, the big drum was contaminated by early research being done in the Chicago stadium for the atomic bomb.

According to Vincent DiNino, long-time Director of Longhorn Bands, General D. Harold Byrd, a prominent Dallas oil man and honorary Longhorn Band president, decided about 1955 to try to locate the big drum because he thought Texas should have the largest drum in the world. DiNino said he thought Byrd paid the University of Chicago one dollar—a token payment—for the drum. Byrd then had it completely renovated and decontaminated and presented it to the Longhorn Band in 1955.

Special doors, approximately 14 feet by 10 feet, in the band hall accommodate Big Bertha. She also has her own trailer to travel to out-of-town games. Getting her into and out of the stadium is usually a big job. She has been the object of numerous pranks—has been slit and hidden away—but she always re-appears.

Her 1974 appearance with the Longhorn Band in the Super Bowl in Houston was one of her "greatest weekends." Other special occasions were her appearance in the inaugural parade of President John F. Kennedy in 1961 and again in the inaugural parade of President Lyndon Johnson in 1964.

The first lady of Texas show business has had a tempestuous career, but she successfully has fended off attacks on her virtue and her life by numerous individuals. She remains the band's sweetheart and the "Biggest Drum in the World."

RUNNING THE FLAG

On January 1, 1962, Texas played the University of Mississippi in the Cotton Bowl and won not only the game (12 to 7), but a huge Texas flag. At half-time, the Rebel Band spelled out "Texas" on the field and then some Mississippi students unfurled a Texas flag, 51 feet wide by 90 feet long, and carried it over the heads of their 96-piece band. The Rebel's own Confederate flag of approximately the same size was then carried over the band, as the field formation was changed from "Texas" to "Dixie." This colorful, dramatic maneuver was performed before a national television audience and the packed Cotton Bowl.

At the end of the half-time ceremonies, Governor Ross Barnett presented the mammoth flag to Governor Price Daniel, who was somewhat astounded by this over-sized gift and later gave it to the Texas Longhorn Marching Band of which Vincent R. DiNino was director.

The big flag was first officially "run" by Texas students the following Thanksgiving when the Band asked members of Alpha Phi Omega (APO), a service fraternity, to "run the flag" as part of the show at the big game with Texas A. & M. The flag was so large that approximately forty men were required to carry and maneuver it across the field. The APO chapter was then given responsibility for complete maintenance and display of the flag.

The original flag was made out of Southern muslin, which was not very durable. Moths and mildew soon left the flag in tatters, even though APO members and their friends repaired it after every game. After five years, the old banner completely disintegrated.

In order to maintain the gala tradition that had developed, APO members and their girl friends made a new flag of roughly the same dimensions. This second Texas flag was carried for a few more years.

At several times during the tenure of the second flag, various viewers suggested that someone should get APO a new flag, one made out of more durable fabric. For seven months, APO president James Flodine worked on getting bids and financial backing for this undertaking. The bid that was finally accepted was submitted by Mrs. Flo Kuehn of Seabrook Sailmakers in Seabrook, Texas. It was Mrs. Kuehn and her assistant, therefore, who constructed the world's largest flag. The Athletics Department paid the bill. The new flag is made exactly like a sail. Seven hundred seventy-seven square yards of four-ounce nylon is bolstered by 800 pound test nylon rope around the perimeter of the flag. This third banner is 37 yards long and 21 yards wide; the star is 27 feet from point to point.

The fall 1972 football season was the first one for the new nylon flag. It has been hung on the stage of Gregory Gymnasium for pep rallies and has been hung on the Main Building for pep rallies and for APO *Cactus* pictures.

The flag is hauled in its own trailer, built and financed by APO. The personalized license plate is "TX FLAG." The flag has been "run" at out-of-town games, such as at the "big shoot-out" in 1969 at Fayetteville when the President of the United States was in attendance, at the Rice game in Houston, at the Baylor game in Waco, at the A. & M. game in College Station, and at the Cotton Bowl in Dallas.

THE OLD WATER TANK

A new 150-foot water tower was erected on the campus before the beginning of the 1904 session. The water shortage caused by the flood and dam break in 1900 led to plans by University officials to provide a water system. The tower, often called Prexy's Pot, became a symbol—a new temptation to class groups desiring to display their numerals.

The old tank, located just south of the Physics building, was the scene of more student gatherings—usually of a rebellious nature—than any other campus landmark. It offered an inviting space on which many different classes could paint their insignia and numerals. When Dr. David F. Houston became President of the University in 1905, he adopted new tactics and told students they could paint the old tank as many times as they desired. After one creative painting splurge, the tank was neglected until Dr. William J. Battle became Acting President and forbade students to touch the tank.

During President Battle's administration, one of the biggest campus fights occurred around the tank. Plans were made as early as December, 1913, to remove it from the campus, because it was not needed. Several years passed, however, before action was taken.

Graduating classes of the School of Aeronautics during World War I even found time to paint their insignia and numerals on the tank.

Finally, early in 1918, a man from Houston paid $2,000 for the landmark. A student reporter lamented, "With the disappearance of the old water tank, the

University loses one of its most cherished and sentimental traditions." *The Daily Texan* editor wrote:

A book might be written on that one tank—in fact, it would take a remarkably large book to contain plates of the various signs painted on the sides of the big cylinder, and we are sure that intervening pages could well be filled. . . .

A student, in a letter to the editor of *The Daily Texan*, wrote:

Our old historic and beloved tank is no more. This old tank was to the University what the Statue of Liberty at the entrance of New York Harbor is to the lover of American democracy. It is the embodiment and emblem of all the splendid traditions, good or bad, of this still more splendid institution.

In a final move, as the old landmark was being oxidized to remove all old paint, the engineers redecorated it again with their insignia.

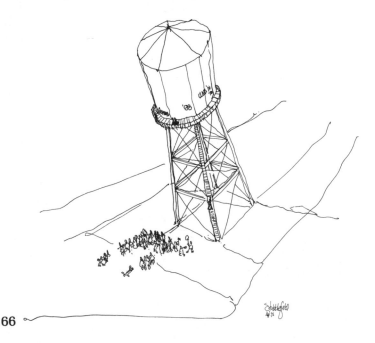

THE SPIRIT OF OLD B. HALL

Few campus buildings have become as intricately interwoven into the sentimental life of the University as old Brackenridge Hall (referred to as B. Hall), which was a four-story dormitory, just east of the Main Building. Opening on December 1, 1890, it had rooms for fifty-eight students and a dining hall for at least one hundred fifty. The rooms were large; each one had a bay window and was furnished with two beds, dresser, bookcase, wardrobe, table and two chairs. Boys in four-room suites shared a bathroom, "supplied at all hours with hot and cold water, and a marble-top washstand with a hydrant attached." Rent at first was $2.50 per month for each student, but it was increased to $3.00 the second year. In rural Texas in the 1890s, young men needed an inexpensive place to live if they attended the University; B. Hall met that need.

In the early days, the one who was manager, director, and cashier of B. Hall was called the "steward." He had problems with the residents because of food, house rules, the heating system, and janitorial service. The students actually preferred to manage the Hall themselves and exerted strong influence over any manager ever appointed.

Two new wings were added in 1900. Finally, governed by its own council, the dormitory "ceased to be a disturbing factor" in University life for a while. It provided an opportunity for improved social conditions among students and helped solve the problems of excessive expenses. For a number of years the Hall was the center of University life for a large number of boys. One professor wrote that the years "from 1900 to 1912 were full of B. Hall affairs, and barely a week passed that some freakish cuss did not spring something entirely original, and not half of it ever got into the magazines or newspapers." A student editor, relating the Hall's history, said it has been called "The Citadel of Democracy" and the "Tammany Hall of the University." A former Governor of Texas, he said, once asserted, "The laws of Texas stop at the doors of B. Hall."

B. Hall was a stronghold for nonfraternity men, because most fraternity men lived in their own houses and were seldom seen at B. Hall. P.E.C.'s, Rusticusses, and GooRoos were organizations formed by some of the residents. They became strong forces in campus politics.

On the eve of March 2 (Texas Independence Day) each year, upperclassmen who lived in the Hall usually expected and quelled an attack by the freshmen. The battle that occurred on March 1, 1925, however, was the last. One student was seriously injured and property damage was over $2,000—a sizable figure at that time. The Legislature was in session when the fight occurred and condemned the action as "barbarous."

On June 28, 1926, President W. M. W. Splawn issued a statement to the effect that B. Hall would be closed to student residents by September because of its proximity to Garrison Hall, a new classroom building, and that the old dormitory would be used for offices. The B. Hall Association immediately filed a suit for an injunction against President Splawn and the Regents to stop plans to make the building into offices. The last resident, who stayed overtime, was "thrown out" at Thanksgiving time, 1926. At a B. Hall banquet in 1925, one resident said:

> Friendships formed in a boy's dormitory are firmer than those made in almost any other place. . . the happiest hours of my University career were spent in B. Hall, and the dearest friendships I have ever made were in B. Hall.

Walter Hunnicutt, director of the Longhorn Band for four years and author of "Texas Fight," was made president of the group to save the building, as he was an ardent champion of preserving the Hall as a dormitory. The crux of the ensuing court battle was whether B. Hall was a trust created by Colonel Brackenridge for poor boys or a gift. The University denied that it was a trust. The Court of Civil Appeals finally ruled that the dormitory was a gift, not a trust. Leaders of the fight vowed their intention to keep the case in court, but in October, 1926, the Board of Regents and former residents—many of whom were prominent in Texas politics—reached a compromise agreement in that a new B. Hall would be built if former residents would raise $100,000 of the necessary funds.

So old B. Hall became an office building and was not torn down until 1952. The new Brackenridge Hall was completed in August, 1932. Students today refer to this building as "old B. Hall," but its history lacks the color and pervasive spirit among former residents that marked the former B. Hall.

On March 16, 1937, a B. Hall reunion was held and those present passed a resolution opposing the Hall's destruction, adopting the slogan, "You may tear down the Alamo, but never B. Hall." Memories of the past were recalled by those who had lived in the old building. They remembered that the Hall was the "Citadel of Democracy"—that bed slats from the Hall had convinced Dr. E. P. Schoch he should direct the Hall's musicians—that more than 4,000 boys had lived there—that stacking a room was a good offset to over-decoration.

On May 30, 1952, Chancellor James P. Hart recommended to the Regents that B. Hall be razed "due to failure in the walls . . . which creates serious hazard of collapse of the structure." The Regents approved the recommendation and in October, 1952, B. Hall came down.

Walter E. Long, wrote an article about B. Hall in 1959 in which he reported the replies of a number of former residents to the question, "Why was B. Hall known as the 'Citadel of Democracy'?" Included were comments such as, "There was no regimentation of the boys living there"; "No class distinction"; "Comradeship"; "Every man expressed himself—all issues fully debated"; "B. Hall was a real factor in making the University what it is today." Truly, a spirit developed among those who lived in—or even knew—old B. Hall that has become a living legend.

SENIOR SWING-OUT AND THE BLUEBONNET CHAIN

Senior Week featured for the first time in 1922 a program called "Swing-Out." Miss Lucy J. Newton, Dean of Women, worked with Cap and Gown, a senior women's group, to plan the ceremony. Even though Senior Week included events for both men and women, Swing-Out was for women only and featured as the major portion of the ceremony a revival of the Bluebonnet Chain tradition that had been started earlier. The Bluebonnet Chain ceremony was first pictured in *The Cactus* in 1917 and showed seniors and juniors of 1916 participating in the simple ceremony. Seniors were in caps and gowns and juniors were in white ankle-length dresses and pointed-toe shoes. Again in 1917, the ceremony was performed on Class Day. Class Day was usually held during Commencement Week in the Teens, and in other ceremonies on that day the president of the senior "Academs" presented the junior president a huge wooden key, symbolic of responsibility. The T-Square of the Engineers, the Peregrinus of the Lawyers, and a Blue-Back Speller from the "Pedoggies" (Education) were ceremoniously presented to the junior representatives on the same occasion. Seniors joined together in a huge book-burning celebration when each one, while marching around a bonfire, tossed in a book.

Miss Lula Mary Bewley, a member of the Dean of Women's staff from 1908 until 1938, recalled that a simple ceremony was performed on Class Day on several occasions before World War I. A member of the Class of 1913 said her class did not have the ceremony, but a member of the Class of 1916 said her class started the ceremony. Real bluebonnets to make

71

a bluebonnet chain were used during the early years. The procession was probably modeled after the idea of the Vassar daisy chain.

The Bluebonnet Chain ceremony was continued during World War I. At the Red Cross Fete of Nations—a wartime replacement in 1918 for the Varsity Circus—"seventy-five girls worked for four hours making 300 feet of bluebonnets embedded in moss." Again, the juniors presented the chain to the seniors that year. All sang "The Eyes of Texas" as the seniors accepted it.

In 1922, when Swing-Out officially began, women from all of the academic classes met on the walks in front of the Main Building about sundown one evening in May. The torch of knowledge was presented to the junior girls, and the senior girls were, in turn, assured the support and loyalty of their successors by means of the bluebonnet chain. Retiring Cap and Gown officials removed their caps and placed them on the heads of the new leaders. Juniors, dressed in white, marched from the Law Building, to music of the Longhorn Band, up paths guarded by freshmen, also dressed in white, to the steps of the Main Building, which sophomores were guarding, and then back down the main walk to await the seniors. The president of Cap and Gown led the seniors who escorted the juniors back up the hill and turned the citadel over to them. The president of the University presented the torch to the president of Cap and Gown, and she passed it on to the new president. Then the seniors marched out, through the protecting bluebonnet chain, into the "outside world." Each year thereafter, the Cap and Gown members passed the bluebonnet chain to the junior women of the University. Approximately 1,000 girls participated in the 1929 ceremony; girls in physical education classes were given a cut from class for taking part in the traditional program.

A Mortar Board chapter was installed in 1923, and after that time members of the senior women's honorary society became an important part of Swing-Out.

A reporter for *The Daily Texan* stated in 1928 that "Due to the biennial nature of the growth of bluebonnets, the sophomores now merely arrange the chain of the paper bluebonnets which were made by sophomore classes of years gone by." Fresh bluebonnets were no longer used.

An outline of the program for 1932 was as follows:

I. March played by the Longhorn Band.
   1. Freshman girls enter to guard the east and west walks in front of the Main Building.
   2. Sophomore girls enter to escort guests.
   3. Junior girls march from Law Building and Sutton Hall to meet Senior girls and receive Bluebonnet Chain.
   4. Senior girls enter carrying Bluebonnet Chain.
II. Ceremonies of Cap and Gown.
   1. Presentation of the Bluebonnet Chain by the Seniors to the Juniors.
   2. Address, given by Miss Ruby Terrell, Dean of Women.
   3. Seniors sing their song to the Juniors.
   4. Announcement of Senior women elected to Phi Beta Kappa.
   5. Presentation of torch to incoming president of Cap and Gown.
   6. Announcement of Cap and Gown Council.
   7. Juniors sing song to Seniors.
   8. Introduction of new Junior president.
   9. Introduction of new Sophomore president.
   10. Presentation of Sophomore scholarship cup by Mortar Board.
   11. Announcement of new members of Mortar Board.
   12. "The Eyes of Texas" by everyone.

13. "T-E-X" played by Band while the Seniors march to east end of the Main Building, where they stand until the Band stops playing; then Seniors sing "T-E-X" without the Band.

Words of the song Juniors sang to the Seniors to the tune of "At Dawning" were:

We gather, dear seniors, to bid you goodbye
And wish you good luck in each task you shall try.
Remember dear Varsity and we who remain
Are bound to you now by the Bluebonnet Chain.

Because the present Main Building was then under construction, the 1935 ceremony was held in front of old B. Hall, near the present location of the Computation Center. In 1936, Swing-Out was held between the Architecture Building and the Old Library Building. The 1937 Swing-Out was the first held in front of the New Main Building. Special guests for the occasion were Governor and Mrs. James V. Allred and Dean H. T. Parlin, who gave the address, "Teaching for Leadership." The giant seal of the University hung from the balcony of the Main Building. Flags were on the poles on the terrace, flowers bedecked the speaker's platform, and a loud-speaker system was arranged. Chairs were available for visitors, and the Longhorn Band played.

During World War II, the ceremony was continued. Captain H. W. Underwood addressed the group in 1942. In 1944, the Tower Chimes played from 6:15 until 6:45 before the ceremony. In that year, June 8 was the date of Swing-Out because of an accelerated University program. Against a background of draped flags, banks of Texas flowers, and the University seal suspended from the second story balcony, the seniors transferred the Bluebonnet Chain to the shoulders of the junior girls as the strains of "Auld Lang Syne" drifted toward Littlefield Fountain. One girl was proclaimed the "Home-front" heroine on the Forty Acres for the month of May and another as chairman of the Campus War Council announced that University girls had accumulated a total of 3,540 hours of volunteer service during the month. U. S. Navy V-12 units preceded the seniors in the march and formed a military guard for the procession. Nurses' aides and Canteen Workers wore their uniforms. These home-front heroines, standing on the steps of the Main Building, gave the Pledge of Allegiance and were congratulated for being in the Red Cross Army of Mercy.

Rain marred the ceremony several times. In 1946, a torrential downpour occurred about fifteen minutes after the program ended. Mrs. Percy V. Pennybacker had been speaker. In 1947, Swing-Out was actually rained out for the first time in its history, but the audience fled to the Texas Union and Mrs. Robert W. Warner, past president of the Austin AAUW, made a speech, honors were announced, and a wet bluebonnet chain was passed over to the Juniors. Two years later, the ceremony was again completed indoors. The president of Cap and Gown introduced Mrs. Rae Files Still, State Representative from the One Hundredth Texas Legislative District. Then the rains came. Mrs. Still continued her short talk in Recital Hall of the Music Building. Rains drove the ceremony to the Union again in 1957, 1959, and 1961.

Mrs. Martin A. Row, president of the Texas League of Women Voters, was speaker in 1950. A *Texan* reporter noted in that year that the Swing-Out ceremony had varied only slightly since 1937.

Recognized annually in the late Forties and early Fifties were the new presidents of Mortar Board, Orange Jackets, UTSA, Campus League of Women Voters, YWCA, Alpha Lambda Delta, Co-Ed Assembly, Panhellenic, Cap and Gown, WICA and House Chairmen. New women members of Phi Beta Kappa,

Mortar Board and Cap and Gown Council were introduced. The Silver Spur Award to the outstanding senior woman was first given in 1953. Also in that year, the orange tower lights were first used during the ceremony. Several scholarships, the Alpha Lambda Delta Book Award and the Mortar Board Scholarship Cup were presented.

Men's organizations were special guests for the first time at Swing-Out on April 29, 1955. Early that spring, Ray Farabee, president of the student body and a member of Silver Spurs, went to the Cap and Gown Council and expressed a desire to make the traditional ceremony one that would honor, in addition to outstanding women leaders, outstanding men leaders of corresponding groups. Cap and Gown decided to invite the men, and Silver Spurs helped with the program. The following men's groups were invited to attend and to be recognized: Inter-fraternity Council, MICA, Men's Co-Op Association, APO, Phi Eta Sigma, Friars, YMCA, UTSA (men), Silver Spurs, and Cowboys. More than twenty mens' and womens' organizations participated in Swing-Out that year. The new student body president, Jerry Wilson, gave greetings, and Diana Klotz was president of Cap and Gown, which still planned the program. Highlight of the program was the announcement of three major honor awards: the Silver Spur cup to the outstanding woman student, the Mike Flynn memorial award to the outstanding man student, and the Marjorie Darilek memorial award to the outstanding independent woman student.

In 1956, the Silver Spurs were invited again to assist Cap and Gown as sponsors, and in 1957, they officially became joint sponsors with Cap and Gown of the thirty-sixth annual Swing-Out. Mr. Ed Price, representing the Dean of Men's office, and Miss Helen Flinn from the Dean of Women's office served as official advisers.

The Seventy-Fifth Anniversary of the University was being celebrated in 1958, and speeches at Swing-Out that year centered around traditions and folklore of the University. An added note of suspense in 1959 was the first public announcement of the name of the new president of the student body. Also presented were the twenty-five students in the recently initiated Junior Fellows program.

In 1961, Swing-Out was dedicated to the honor of the late Dean of Men, Dr. Carl V. Bredt, who had died on April 1. The 1962 Swing-Out was dedicated to the late Joe C. (Jodie) Thompson of Dallas, a prominent ex-student and member of the Board of Regents from 1957 until his death in 1961.

A student editor wrote, in 1958, in *The Daily Texan*:

> Traditions, we believe, are a significant part of the life at any university. And at The University of Texas, too often we tend to ignore our links with the past as we go from day to day in a mad rush, involved only in the immediate campus whirl.
>
> Tonight, at 7 p.m., Swing-Out, one of the University's finest traditional events, will unfold once more on the Main Building Terrace. Swing-Out—a ceremony for recognition of student leadership, and more important, a symbol of the transferring of that leadership from the old order to the new order.

During the 1960s, however, students tended to rebel against traditions and desired to change or abolish ceremonies that were in any way traditional. Swing-Out and the Bluebonnet Chain were victims. The 1963 ceremony, therefore, was the last.

TEA-SIPPERS

"Tea-Sippers" is a label scoffingly given U. T. Austin students and ex-students by those who did not attend U. T. The Aggies originated the term years ago. The real reason for the insulting nickname has been disputed, but several theories exist.

In the early years, U. T. had the reputation of being a "country-club" school, and Tea-Sippers was an appropriate label for "members of the club"—those who sat around in the big fraternity houses and sipped "tea."

One theory is that the "Hook 'em, 'Horns" sign called to Aggie minds the act of daintily holding a tea cup with the little finger sticking out. Of course, Texas Exes dating beyond 1950 know that the insulting label had been used long before the "Hook 'em" signal was introduced.

"Tea-Sippers" was a "sissy" term compared to "Aggies," so Aggies began saying the big Texas "T" stood for "Tea-Sips." One Texas-Ex remembers an old version of the Aggie War Hymn that went something like this:

> T is for Texas U?
> Hellno!
> T is for Tea-Sippers!
> Hulla-balloo, Hulla-balloo
> Caneck, Caneck, etc.
>
> . . .
>
> Goodbye to Texas Univer-si-tee, etc.

JUDGE CLARK
CHRISTMAS DINNERS

James B. Clark was auditor, comptroller, dean, registrar, librarian, secretary to the faculty, and caretaker of the campus. His official title was Proctor and Librarian. He served from the year the University opened in 1883 until he died suddenly on December 8, 1908.

The event for which Judge Clark became well known was the annual Christmas dinner, which bore his name. He started the dinners in 1887 when he invited to lunch several boys who could not afford to go home for Christmas. After a traditional meal of turkey and dressing, they sat around a tree decorated with strings of popcorn and cranberries, sang songs, told stories, and forgot their homesickness.

Judge Clark explained his reason for inviting the boys to dinner: "There is always hope for a young man as long as he loves his home, or, if he has none, so long as he cherishes its memories and associates. The haggard witches of temptation may gather round him, but so long as are kept alive the endeavoring influences of early home life, there is home."

The following year, approximately 10 to 20 percent of the male students were staying on campus. This number was too large to have at his home; so Judge Clark arranged, at his own expense, for a traditional meal to be served in the old B. Hall cafeteria. Hence, the tradition was born; every Christmas until his death in 1908, he served as host and toastmaster at what became known as the Judge Clark Dinner.

Often the dinners would last up to five hours. Not only would the food be good and plentiful, but all kinds of stunts were performed and stories were told. Guests traditionally assembled in the B. Hall dining room at 2:30, and after the meal, students filled the room with cigar smoke and toasts. It was customary for the University president to respond to the first toast. Then each guest was called upon for a speech. The group sang and gave yells before departing.

After Judge Clark's death, the custom of providing Christmas dinner was reinstated through the efforts of B. Hall Manager Seary and Dr. George P. Garrison. Other professors helped with the celebration. Judge John C. Townes, Professor T. U. Taylor, and Dr. H. Y. Benedict were often called upon.

In December 1913, the Judge Clark Christmas Dinner moved to the sponsorship of the University Y, and the renewal of the "time-honored tradition" was met with enthusiasm. In 1916 the "monster turkey dinner for the men" was scheduled for the Tuesday after Christmas. By 1917, it was customary for the Y to begin the dinner at 7:30 on Christmas Eve, and students who wished to attend were requested to sign cards so the committee would know how many to expect.

By 1932, the Christmas dinner, with its "traditional savory and colorful food, good fellowship, Christmas tales and Christmas carols," had become the center of Christmas spirit and Christmas cheer for those whose family centers were too far away for their presence in the flesh. That year guests from Mexico, Cuba, the Canal Zone, and at least 12 states in the United States attended.

In the late thirties, the number of students who remained in Austin over the holidays became so small that the Judge Clark dinners were discontinued, according to Dr. C. Richard King in an *Alcalde* article, and the tradition honoring the man who had been recognized as "the only man on the campus who had the full confidence of the students, faculty, the public, and the regents" became a thing of the past.

MARCH 2 CELEBRATION

Celebration of Texas Independence Day at U. T. Austin began in grand style in 1897. University students asked for a holiday so they could celebrate the signing of the Declaration of Independence of Texas 61 years before in Noah Byer's blacksmith shop on a cold morning.

President G. T. Winston, who had just come to Texas from the University of North Carolina, refused the students' request. In fact, Winston told them that the only day he was going to celebrate was July 4 and reminded the persistent law students that Texas was a part of the United States.

Not to be brushed off, the senior law students, headed by "Snakey Jones" (J. S. Jones, then an end of the varsity football squad and later an attorney at Bastrop) and joined by most of the juniors, went to the Capitol grounds and "proceeded to exercise their inalienable right to liberty and the pursuit of happiness." They "borrowed" a cannon and took it back to the campus, where they celebrated the rest of the day. Tom Connally, dressed in a black hat and black tie and wearing a "Borah" haircut, was head cannoneer, although he was only a junior law student. He set off the shots that hurtled down University Avenue. Frank R. Newton of San Antonio was the ramrod. Others recalled by Judge A. N. Moursund in 1936 as being participants in the 1897 action were Will Hogg, W. W. McCrory, J. W. McClendon, and Pat Neff.

81

Firing began with such intensity that it shattered some windows in the Main Building. The boys were ordered to remove the cannon. Later, when everything was becoming quiet, a roar was heard from Clark Field. The "sons of liberty" were at it again! During the firing, which had drawn out the entire student body of 400, the would-be-lawyers engaged in oratory that later made them famous.

President Winston finally decided to join the group and made his famous speech that has become a tradition:

I was born in the land of liberty, rocked in the cradle of liberty, nursed on the bottle of liberty, and I've had liberty preached to me all my life, but Texas University students take more liberty than anyone I've ever come in contact with.

Another tradition originating from that first Independence Day at the University was an annual fight between freshmen and sophomores, which usually included a pushball contest. The tradition ended when famous old B. Hall was severely damaged in a friendly fracas in 1925.

As early as 1904, March 2 became a day for ex-students to observe as a holiday. Even today, wherever two or more exes are gathered together, they celebrate.

University students on the campus continued to mark the occasion by gathering on the South Mall to watch a cannon be fired at 11:45 a.m. The ceremony included a five-minute concert by the Longhorn Band and the raising of the Texas flag. In 1951, the Kappa Sigma fraternity members dressed themselves as Mexicans and returned the cannon fire from their big house, which then sat in a direct line of fire from the Main Building. This tradition was continued until the late sixties, when some groups charged racial prejudice.

82

MEMORIAL STADIUM

The idea for Texas Memorial Stadium, long a dream of athletics director L. Theo Bellmont, was actually born when a small group of students held a meeting in the fall of 1923. At a general meeting of the student body a short time later, students decided that the University should have a stadium. The idea was presented to the Regents in December, 1923. Early in 1924, the Regents appointed a central committee to be in charge of stadium affairs. On this committee were representatives of the student body, the faculty, the ex-students, the Regents, the Athletic Council, Austin business men, and businessmen of the state.

The Stadium Committee held its first meeting in January, 1924, and decided to incorporate the stadium in order that its business affairs might be more easily managed. H. J. Lutcher Stark was chosen president of the corporation. The stadium was to be a statewide memorial to all the Texas men and women who served in World War I. On November 12, 1977, it was rededicated "in memory of all American veterans of all wars."

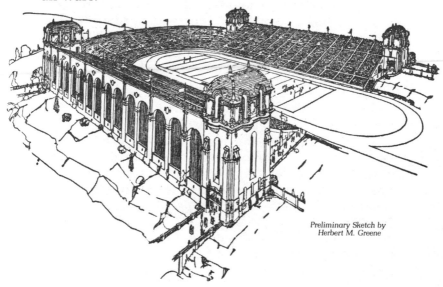

Preliminary Sketch by
Herbert M. Greene

The first campaign for funds was held on the campus by students. Under the leadership of William L. McGill, an organization of about 400 students was formed, and after a week of intensive campaigning, the students had raised $151,000. Mr. and Mrs. Lutcher Stark added ten percent to this amount, making the campus total $166,000.

The next campaign was held in the City of Austin and was conducted by business men and women under the leadership of Sam Sparks. After a week, Austin citizens had subscribed $115,000.

The campaign spread out into other cities in the state during the spring, summer, and fall. In the fall, the new student group decided they wanted a part in the movement and subscribed $36,000.

The contract for building the east and west stands of the stadium was let in the spring of 1924, and the work was rushed to completion with all possible speed. The structure was dedicated on Thanksgiving Day, 1924—one year and two days after the first student meeting at which the idea was introduced. The original goal set for the campaign was $500,000 by Thanksgiving Day, 1924. When pledges were totaled, $505,000 had been subscribed.

The first unit of the stadium consisted of the east and west stands with a seating capacity of 27,000. Approximately 33,000 people attended the dedication ceremonies in 1924, and temporary bleachers had to be erected to accommodate the overflow crowd. The new student group in 1925 started a movement to build the horseshoe curve in the north end of the stadium. They staged a campaign and subscribed $27,000 for this purpose. The 1926 class kept the drive going and raised the pledge total for the whole stadium project to $554,716, of which only $371,166 had actually been collected, according to a spring accounting. The completion of the north horseshoe section in 1926 raised the seating to 40,500.

Plans called for the addition of seats on the two sides that would raise the capacity to 50,000 and the building of four ornamental towers at the ends of the east and west sides. This last phase was never accomplished, and two decades passed before the stadium was enlarged again. A large plaque with names of Texans killed in World War I was erected on top of the north stands several years later.

A $1,500,000 expansion in 1948 lifted the permanent seating capacity to over 60,000 and the maximum, with bleachers, to 66,000.

Late in October, 1969, construction began on another expansion project. At a Regents' meeting in November, 1965, the Board had voted not to move Memorial Stadium to another location. The new addition included an 11-story building under a new west upper deck. This new upper deck seats an additional 16,000 spectators, bringing the total seating capacity of Memorial Stadium to approximately 81,000 when bleachers are placed in the south end. The cost of the new addition created some controversy. Originally scheduled to cost $12,800,000, the final figure for the new upper deck, the 11-story building, a new press box and other stadium improvements, was considerably more. The cost was partially funded through the sale of 10-year seat options to Longhorn fans for $400, $300, and $200 per seat. After a number of delays, the upper deck was first used during the 1972 football season. The adjacent classroom building which houses physical education facilities, faculty offices, intercollegiate athletic affairs, and the U. T. police department, was opened later in 1972.

AstroTurf was first installed in the stadium in 1969 at a cost of $525,000. Continued use of the field, both during and after football season, caused the artificial grass to wear down, and new AstroTurf was installed in 1974.

U. T. VS.
TEXAS A. & M.

No University tradition through the years has been more colorful than the annual football game, usually on Thanksgiving Day, between Texas and Texas A. & M.

The first game between these two schools was played in 1894 with Texas winning 38 to 0. In 1911, when the game was being played in Houston, the A. & M. students were dissatisfied with the score of 6-0 in favor of Texas and literally tore into the victorious Longhorns. Because of the tension between the two teams, the annual games were discontinued until 1915.

Texas Memorial Stadium was built in 1924, and Texas A. & M. did not win a game in it until 1956.

One of the memorable ceremonies associated with the annual gridiron tussle has been the spirit that erupts at the big pep rally and bonfire preceding the game. At Texas, the Cowboys sponsor the collection of wood for the bonfire, and a contest is usually staged to see which organization can gather the most wood. The winner is given a cup.

It was not unusual for the Aggies to attempt to set the fire prematurely. In 1948, U. T. students "bombed" the A. & M. bonfire from an airplane. Organizations often went too far in securing wood. One fraternity once had to return 340 vegetable crates and 300 crate lids stolen from an Austin market. Telephone and electric light poles were often misused. A number of confiscated outhouses, in the days when they were used, had to be returned.

Freshman Field was the site of the annual bonfire for a number of years until the Athletic Council ruled it out because nails and glass were dangerous for players. Pease Park has been used. Both the south and north banks of the Colorado River (now Town Lake) have been the site of the bonfire. The most recent location is east of Interstate 35 near U.S. 290.

Although the games are not designated as homecoming games by either school, they have become just that. The stadiums are always full of students and alumni who return from all over the state and nation for the big game. Many of the exes still have reunions on the day of the game, which is usually televised by one of the national networks.

THE PATRON SAINTS

Alexander Fredericke Clair

The patron saint of the engineers, Alexander Fredericke Clair, existed only in song from 1902 until 1908. In 1902, Edward Cowan Connor brought to the campus the words of a song extolling his virtues that was set to the tune of "Frau Diavilo."

A small group of carousing sophomore engineers stopped at Jacoby's Beer Garden early on April Fool's Day, 1908. While at the Garden, one of the engineers spotted a wooden statue of a little fat-bellied fellow about five feet high holding aloft a glass of beer in his right hand. Dean T. U. Taylor of the Engineering School claimed that while one of the group engaged Mr. Jacoby in conversation, the other members slipped the statue out. But one member of the group later insisted that they obtained Mr. Jacoby's permission to borrow the statue for a few days. On that same day, the engineers met in front of the Main Building with the statue. At an intermission between classes, Joe H. Gill presented the statue to the assembled engineers as their Patron Saint and traced his ancestry back to the Pyramids, the Hanging Gardens of Babylon, and the aqueducts of Rome.

Alf Toombs finished the job a year later on April 1, 1909, when he unveiled the statue again in front of the Main Building, christened him "Alexander Fredericke Clair," (from the 1902 ballad) and, in an eloquent speech, traced his ancestry back to the Garden of Eden.

So it was that the Patron Saint of the Texas Engineers began his reign. For a while, Alec was placed at the head of the steps on the first floor of the Engineering Building, the present Dean of Students Office. On March 3, 1910, a group of law students stole Alec, but Judge Townes stepped in and ordered the students to return him. He was returned on March 31, 1910. But this episode was only the beginning of Alec's odyssey.

He was stolen again in 1913 and in 1916, each time being recovered after long searches. In the fall of 1918, during World War I, engineering students cut the right leg of old Alec into small strips and branded the pieces "Celafotrap" ("part-of-Alec" spelled backwards). A piece was sent to all Texas engineers serving in France. This deed called for a replacement. A new Alec was obtained in 1919, and the old one was retired to a "Mountain Ranch."

On February 21, 1927, the new Alec was captured by the lawyers and cut into pieces. On March 1, of that same year, his head was returned to Dean T. U. Taylor by then Governor Dan Moody.

In the spring of 1928, old Alec was brought back from his "Mountain Ranch," and restored to service. At various times, he was stored in a barn in Webberville, under a stack of wood cases in a Coca-Cola plant in Giddings, in a cellar in Dallas, and in Charlottesville, Virginia. In 1936, he was returned to a closet in Taylor Hall. He resided peacefully in Texas Memorial Museum for several years.

Journalism students found him in a house on Archway Street in 1964. That same year he made his first public appearance in 25 years at a reunion during the college's celebration of the University's 80th anniversary. He posed for pictures with several local old-timers in 1971. In 1972 and 1973, he appeared on the platform during the college's Honors Day convocations.

Ironically, Alec was kidnapped by law students three times in two days after his 1973 appearance. Through all his escapades, Alec has kept his dignity and has shown an amazing capacity for resurrection and survival. Engineers are assured that "Alec is alive and well!"

Peregrinus

Jim McCall of Weatherford was center on the famous football team of 1900. Because of his football interests, Jim missed some of his law classes. He was absent from class on the day that Judge W. S. Simkins lectured on the Peregrinus (Perry-grine-us), the old traveling Justice of the Peace of the Roman Empire. Jim knew nothing about the Peregrinus when Judge Simkins asked him to recite.

"Judge, I don't know what it was unless it was some kind of an animal." This response brought a roar of laughter. Russell Savage, another student in the class, drew a picture of his concept of "the animal" while Scott Key watched to see that Judge Simkins did not catch him. The picture remained on the board several days and provoked many hearty laughs.

Jim McCall withdrew from the University at the end of the fall term and did not return to the University, but it was he who gave Russell Savage the idea for the animal that was to become the Patron Saint of the Laws.

In the spring of 1901, Savage, aided by Elmer Pope, redrew the Peregrinus on a pattern, cut it out of cloth, and his landlady sewed this pattern on a background of cloth. The whole sheet was then attached to two staffs.

90

Perry, this "Star of the East," has the tail of a fox, pointing out his foxiness; the body of a donkey, denoting indomitable determination; the head of a stork, foretelling the generations of lawyers to come; the eyes of an eagle, which shows keenness; the bill of a lawyer, proving his ability. The lawyers claim that he stands for all that makes a man great: Pep, Power, and Pertinacity.

Judge Simkins explained that the nondescript animal symbolizes both in limb and attitude the maxims in equity that guide the administration of the system. "For instance," he said, "on one of the front feet as originally drawn was an Irish ditcher's boot—indicating the law's protection to the least of mankind. On the other front foot were naked claws, indicating that the greatest of mankind must fear its power. The arched back in the attitude of springing, indicated that the law was ever ready to protect right or prevent wrong. The sharp beak indicated the power to penetrate the mysteries of law which the true student must obtain by study. The bushy tail indicated that Equity brushes away the technicalities of the law and does justice to the merits."

In the spring of 1912, the banner of Perry was taken from the Law Building by five senior engineers and by one academic. It was cut into six pieces and sent in six different directions. That fall, another Perry was constructed. Not only was a banner made, but a papier mache figure was created.

Perry's history has been one of intrigue and excitement. In 1930, some students captured the wooden Perry between the American National Bank and the Driskill Hotel and destroyed it. Two of the group were tried in District Court for contempt but were exonerated.

Today, Perry still presides—in body and in spirit—as Patron Saint of all Texas law students.

Hermes

Hermes, symbol of success and efficiency, is a statue with winged sandals, an emblem of swiftness. He has a bag of gold, representing a trophy of his successful commercial transactions. He has a staff entwined with serpents, serving as an emblem of his wisdom and authority in all strategic negotiations. An eagle sits at his feet. Hermes to Business Administration students is considered as a symbol of success and efficiency in business enterprise.

Ptah

Ptah, Patron Saint of the Architects, was a sculptor or engraver, and he was the chief handicraftsman in metal and stone. He was the greatest of all the Memphis gods and is often regarded as the personification of the rising sun just as it appears over the eastern horizon and also as the opening of the day.

Ptah is represented as a bearded man with a bald head, often dressed in skin tight clothes. From the back of the neck swings a pendant, and in his hand is a scepter. When standing, he is posed in front of an obelisk which symbolizes stability. He is credited with wondrous deeds and achievements.

At U. T., students have declined to design any representative or image of Ptah. He is called upon at various occasions to appear, and he assumes different shapes. The architects call upon him but do not expect him to appear in person. They expect his spirit to protect them.

PUSHBALL CONTEST

The pushball was an enormous leather-covered sphere that was approximately six feet in diameter. It was brought early to the playing field in a conveyance and thereafter guarded carefully by juniors and seniors who acted as marshals for the big contests between freshmen and sophomores.

On Texas Independence Day, March 2, the freshmen and sophomores usually had an annual pushball contest. It would be the climax of a frenetic period that began at dusk the day before and consisted of mass assaults on B. Hall, the stronghold of the upperclassmen, and in various abductions, gauntlet runnings, head-shavings, and syrup-and-featherings.

On the field, the freshmen were distinguished by lampblack on their foreheads and cheeks. They would mill restlessly in a group in one section of the field. The sophomores, equally restive, were similarly grouped about 30 yards away. The ball squatted between them.

The purpose of the contest was literally to push the ball, at a given signal, across a goal line near either end of the field. With students massed on opposite sides, there wasn't much movement at the outset, but soon the ball would rise from out of the tangle; riding high on the many hands, it would begin traveling in one direction or the other toward a goal.

Certainly this would seem an innocuous pastime, yet it could be exciting after the first five minutes. The marshals counted off an equal number of contestants from either side to start the game, but if the tide turned ever so slightly to favor the freshmen, additional sophomores would be slipped into the contest. This action would be noted by the opposition, who, with howls of anguish and dismay, would break quickly through the marshals and come charging up the field. At this point, less than a dozen might be pushing the ball and some 50 or more would be engaged in fist fights and wrestling matches, or just sitting on one another. The noise was terrific with all the shouting and laughing. Most men wore caps in those days, and they would often throw them into the air. These caps were truly the relics of the battlefield and would later appear on the heads of neighborhood boys, sometimes so ill-fitting that they sagged below the ears.

"In spite of the strenuosity that marked the push-ball contest, I don't believe I ever saw a student seriously hurt; nor, for that matter, can I remember one who appeared angry or pugnacious. It was a rough but hilarious sport," one observer of these events recalled.

When the ball itself seemed to be abandoned in the general free-for-all, the marshals somehow managed to restore order and the contest proceeded. The score was usually 2-1 or 2-0, and the sophomores always won.

LITTLEFIELD FOUNTAIN

The Littlefield Memorial Fountain was turned on for the first time on March 26, 1933. It was part of the Littlefield Memorial Entrance Gate, a gift of Major George W. Littlefield, and was designed by Pompeo Coppini and arranged in place by consulting architect, Paul P. Cret.

The fountain and six statues standing between it and the Main Building, four along the South Mall and two on the Lower Terrace, made up the Memorial. An inscription on the west wall of the fountain tersely identifies Major Littlefield: "Soldier in the Confederate Army, leader in Texas Industry, Regent of the University."

Another inscription describes the intention of the Memorial:

> To the men and women of the Confederacy who fought with valor and suffered with fortitude that states' rights be maintained, and who, not dismayed by defeat nor discouraged by misrule, builded from the ruins of a devastating war a greater South, and to the men and women of the Nation who gave of their possessions and of their lives that free government be made secure to the peoples of the earth, this memorial is dedicated.

The fountain consists of three concentric pools on different levels with jets of water spraying on a bronze group, representing Columbia returning victorious from World War I. On the prow of a ship stands a woman of heroic size holding in her right hand the Torch of Light, in her left hand the Palm of Victory. On one side a stalwart lad represents the Army. In front of the ship, three sea horses, two of them ridden by Tritons, symbolize the surging ocean. In the wall back of the group is a bronze door leading

to the underground pumps that drive the water. On this door is a dedicatory inscription to those "sons and daughters of the University of Texas" who gave their lives in World War I. Names of 97 are listed.

On the wall to the east and west of the door are quotations from Cicero carved in the original international Latin words to show the honor given to patriotism by all ages in all lands.

Statues in the group are those of John H. Reagan, James Stephen Hogg, Woodrow Wilson, Robert E. Lee, Albert Sidney Johnston, and Jefferson Davis. (The statue of George Washington was erected later by the Daughters of the American Revolution in the State of Texas.)

President Vinson described the meaning of the memorial:

> The conception in the minds of the architects and sculptor of the Littlefield Memorial is the setting forth of the Division which existed in American life practically from the beginning of the history of this Republic, and which found its climactic expression in the Civil War, the result of which was to destroy the cause of the previous division and to furnish the opportunity through which national life in the future might become fused into one complete whole. The gate, however, is intended to express the thought that this fusion was not complete until the Army and Navy of the United States crossed the Atlantic Ocean in the Great War of 1917 and 1918, and when men from the North and South and the East and West fought shoulder to shoulder for the deliverance of Europe and the world from autocracy. For this reason, everything in the gate converges upon the heroic group in the center. Jefferson Davis of the Confederacy and Woodrow Wilson of the reunited nation, with Lee and Johnston, and Hogg and Reagan, are all grouped as a court of honor about this central figure of a united and victorious America, drawn by two seahorses across the ocean to aid in giving Democracy its place in civilization.

J. Frank Dobie, Southwestern folklorist and University professor, once remarked:

> It is a conglomeration of a woman standing up with arms and hands that look like stalks of Spanish daggers, horses with wings on their feet aimlessly ridden by some sad figure of the male sex and of various other paraphernalia.

During World War II, Dobie suggested selling the fountain for scrap metal to assist the war effort.

Pompeo Coppini defended his work of art by explaining:

> The center horse, riderless, represents the uncontrolled emotional forces of mob hysteria,while the remaining two horses controlled by their riders depict the value of manpower.

Costing $250,000 in 1932, Littlefield Fountain has been, through the years, the host of many pinning parties and pledge dunkings. Many strange items have turned up in the pool. Ducks and even alligators have been found in the waters. Many times it has frothed and foamed when boxes of detergent or bubble bath were added.

Recirculating water pumped by 20-horsepower electric motors at the rate of 3,000 gallons a minute has provided the scene for numerous campus pranks. In the spring of 1973, Littlefield Fountain, as well as other fountains on the campus, were cut off for an indefinite period because of the nationwide energy crisis. All fountains were turned on again in September, 1974.

THE MUSTANGS

Photographed almost as often as the University Tower is the statuary group known as "The Mustangs." Located in front of Texas Memorial Museum, the group consists of a stallion, five mares, and a colt as they scramble down the side of a mountain.

The late A. Phiminster Proctor, one of the greatest sculptors of western life, was selected to create the statue. He was recommended by J. Frank Dobie, former University professor and famous Southwest folklorist. Proctor had gained national fame through such works as the "Princeton Tigers" at Princeton, the "Pioneer Mother" at Kansas City and a statue of "Rough Rider." He worked two and one-half years creating the mustang group.

Ralph R. Ogden, Austin oilman and cattleman who was killed in an Oklahoma automobile collision in 1944, was the man behind the monument. He was unable to interest others in the project, so he donated the necessary $60,000 himself.

The first model for the mustangs was made in Seattle, Washington. It was only about a foot long and was done in plastolene. After Ogden had seen and approved the model, Proctor was invited to do the actual sculpturing at the King Ranch, near Kingsville, Texas. He was given the use of a cabin and a large shelter where he could work.

Plaster casts of the statue were made and sent to the Gorham Company of Providence, R.I. in 1941 for casting in bronze. Because bronze was a vital war metal, the mustang group was stored until the fall of 1947, when work was resumed. The bronze casting was completed in 1948, and the statue was shipped to Austin. Special problems in shipping were caused by the size and weight of the monument.

Cast as a single unit, the hollow bronze group weighs ten tons and stands fifteen feet above its base. Because it was three feet too high to clear overhead bridges and tunnels, the stallion's head had to be removed for shipment on the flatcar. The statue was eighteen inches wider than the flatcar, so one section of the base, with the colt, had to be separated for the trip.

A $10,000 excavation project prepared the base for the statue, which was unveiled at Commencement Exercises in 1948. Proctor, 87 years of age by that time, was present for the event. Mrs. Ethel Ogden, the donor's widow, also attended the ceremonies.

The freedom, the grace, and the beauty of the horses provide a fitting tribute to the tough, fast, intelligent animals that played so great a part in taming the West.

ANNUAL CHRISTMAS CAROL PROGRAM

The annual Christmas carol program was started in 1924. It was co-sponsored by the City of Austin until 1939. From then until 1973, the University continued the event.

In 1940, a lighted tree was placed on the balcony of the Main Building by Arthur Brandon, former public relations director for the University. The Longhorn Band, with its leader, Colonel George E. Hurt, dressed as Santa Claus, played carols.

The singing of Christmas carols, with words flashed on screens placed on the front of the Main Building, the reading of the Christmas story from St. Luke, and the presentation of living carols usually made up the program. University choral groups would take part in the program, and the University president would usually make a short speech. A large audience would gather on the mall to participate in the program.

In 1973, the program was discontinued. Because fall semester classes ended early in December, many students left for home early and others were busy taking exams or studying for them. Criticism began to come, too, for the University's active participation in a religious ceremony. A determined grounds crew, however, put up a tree anyway. No lights were placed on it because of the energy crisis, but the tree was covered with artificial icicles.

THE DAILY TEXAN

On the University campus, early student publications did not receive a hearty welcome from faculty members. The faculty objected to the first attempt, made privately, in 1883 to publish a University magazine. Several other early attempts also failed. Finally, *The Ranger*, a paper started in 1900, and *The Calendar*, a weekly journal published in 1889 and again in 1899-1900, combined, and only one paper, *The Texan*, was published in the fall of 1900. The first four volumes were published as a private enterprise; from volume five onward, *The Texan* was published by the Students' Association until the Texas Student Publications, Inc., was chartered in May, 1921.

The Texan became a semiweekly in September, 1907, and then became a daily, by student referendum, in the fall of 1913. Before a vote was taken during the preceding semester, the student editor urged adoption of a daily, because the increased number of dodgers, posters, and bulletins had become a nuisance. The editor-in-chief and managing editor, as in the past, were elected by students at large.

When the School of Journalism opened in September, 1914, the student publications remained independent of the school itself, but improved preparation of editors and reporters was one reason for establishing the school.

Student publications had financial problems during the Teens. The new Blanket Tax, adopted in 1916, allocated a part of the optional student activity fee to

The Daily Texan. Financial problems continued to plague the publications. The Students' Association finally requested a 50-year charter from the State of Texas for Texas Student Publications, Inc. The charter was granted in May, 1921. The management of affairs of this corporation was vested in a board of nine members—two selected by and from the Students' Assembly, three faculty members appointed by the President of the University, the President of the Students' Association, and the editors of the official student publications. The board annually elected a supervising business manager who had sole power of direction and general supervision of official publications.

In 1925, after twenty-five years of publication, the student paper claimed to have the largest staff of reporters of any newspaper in the world. One hundred and sixty-five students had positions on the student paper!

A thrust for independence has been a noticeable characteristic of student editors since *The Texan* began publication. Changing emphases in make-up of publication, in editorial policies, and in value of news as measured by its location in the paper tended to reflect student interest and attitudes through the years. Editors have periodically protested violations of the inviolable right of freedom of the press. They have complained of censorship and have criticized discipline committees and administrators for attempting to regulate the content of *The Daily Texan.* A review of the publication through the years indicates that not many volumes escaped the editors' complaints about attempts at censorship.

The TSP charter was amended several times before it expired in 1971. An attempt to renew the charter by the TSP Board of Directors was blocked. Following a considerable amount of discussion, legal counsel, debate, and threatened litigation, the corporation was dissolved and a Declaration of Trust, offered by the Regents of the U. T. System, was accepted by the TSP Board of Directors. The new agreement permitted the TSP Board to serve as "Operating Trustees" of the assets and publications of the former Texas Student Publications, Inc. Under the terms of the Trust, the publications of TSP are operated by the University, all employees are employed by the University, and the ultimate authority governing the individual publications of TSP collectively rests with the University.

The new Board of Trustees is composed of four students from the School of Journalism who are elected within the school; two undergraduate students elected at-large in campus-wide elections; two journalism faculty members and one business administration faculty member appointed by the U. T. Austin President; and two professional journalists, also appointed by the President. Voting board members total eleven. Ex officio, nonvoting members include the General Manager of Student Publications, the Dean of Students or his delegate, the Editorial Manager of *The Daily Texan*, and the student editors of all TSP publications.

TSP now has its own building and equipment within the new Communications complex. The *Texan* has a well-designed, beautiful suite of offices and laboratories, and it has a new press.

The editor of the *Texan* is still elected by the student body, and beginning in September, 1974, students indicated their willingness to support the paper through payment of optional fees.

The Daily Texan has often been an award-winning paper and is nationally recognized as one of the finest university newspapers being published.

THE CACTUS

The student yearbook, *The Cactus*, first appeared in 1894. The first volume, with barely 100 pages, was illustrated only by group pictures of each class and one photograph of the Capitol, but it was filled with poetry, prose, and history.

The Cactus was first published by the senior classes, then by the fraternities, by classes again, and in 1899 the Athletic Association began publishing it. In 1912, the Students' Association took over the task.

Realizing that something had to be done to organize the jumbled affairs of the separate student publications, the Students' Association obtained a state charter creating Texas Student Publications, Inc., in May 1921, and the corporation began publishing *The Daily Texan, The Cactus,* and *The Longhorn.* Other publications were later added. The new form of management, chartered for fifty years, proved to be "a business-like, well-managed, money-making organization." Each year the profits earned were turned into improving the publications.

The Cactus continued to please the majority of students. The 1923 book was awarded third place among college yearbooks of America, and the 1924 book won honorable mention. The "grind" section, or "Cactus Thorn," often drew criticism, but the editors continued to act independently.

The depression years did not noticeably affect *The Cactus.* The size of each volume was between four and five hundred pages. The cost of production of the 1932 yearbook was $25,000. Improvements were obvious in lay-out, art work, representation, and photography.

Dolph Briscoe, Jr., was editor of Volume 50, the first book with war as a theme. During the forties, flags, eagles, battleships, and excessive use of red, white and blue characterized the books.

The fifties were fun, and *The Cactus* reflected that feeling. Little notice was given to national issues. The Korean War was thousands of miles away; so the editors of *The Cactus* concentrated on the Forty Acres. During the fifties a supervisor, whose job was to see that the yearbook was managed in a business-like manner, was appointed. The supervisor was to be responsible to the general manager of TSP.

The Cactus improved even more in the sixties. The 1962, 1963, and 1964 issues all won Second-Class ratings from the Associated Collegiate Press (ACP). Also, in 1962, *The Cactus* won the Publication Industries of America (PIA) award, an honor given to only a few books. The 1965, 1966, 1967, 1969, and 1970 issues received First Class ratings from ACP, but the 1968, 1971, 1972, and 1973 issues received "All American" ACP ratings. The 1971 issue received "All American" with four marks of distinction from ACP and also won the Printers' Industries of America award. The 1972 and the 1974 issues received the "All American" with four marks of distinction. The 1973 issue won "All American" with five marks of distinction, the highest honor any yearbook can win.

As these awards may indicate, the U. T. yearbook has changed with the times. Campus life is beautifully portrayed, color is used generously, and photography has become professional. The 1974 issue omitted the Bluebonnet Belles and the Ten Most Beautiful—another change reflecting societal influences. The 1977 budget was $156,600, and *The Cactus* office in the new Communications Building is beautiful as the staff deserves!

In 1971, when the charter of Texas Student Publications, Inc., expired, a trust was formed to replace the corporation, and publication of *The Cactus* was not interrupted. In 1974, student support of TSP became optional, and *The Cactus* now faces the uncertainties of continuing financial solvency. Time will tell how much student support *The Cactus* has.

106

THE BLUNDERBUSS

Through the years, certain "unofficial" publications have appeared—often to the consternation of the administration and to the delight of students. In the '60s, the *Rag* began publication and its distribution on campus was finally resolved after a court battle.

The Blunderbuss, however, which first appeared on campus on April 1, 1914, was the pacesetter for these "unofficial" publications. The unknown editors explained on the masthead, "Our policy may be a little saffron hued, but we love to hear the hypocrite howl when the whitewash gets barked. More bricks, Adolphus."

The first edition of *The Blunderbuss* left most faculty members feeling indifferent, but Mrs. Helen Marr Kirby, Dean of Women, seized two hundred and fifty copies. *The Daily Texan* editor wrote, "*The Blunderbuss* is a journalistic venture foreign to *The Daily Texan*. . . . Be a good sport. Take a joke." A letter in the Firing Line contained these words: "I think those who printed *The Blunderbuss* should be punished. . . ." Thus was born a controversial publication that was to become even more controversial as it appeared each April 1 for a number of years.

In 1915, the *'Buss* was printed tabloid size on yellow and green paper. Bolder and more outspoken than its predecessor, the 1915 edition continued to burlesque and increased its popularity by including some sexy articles.

Faculty action was not taken until after the 1917 *'Buss* appeared. The editors used World War I as its theme and claimed that wireless radios were "discovered" among University professors of German ancestry.

In 1918, two papers were published — *The Blunderbuss*, on April 1, and *The Blunderbustle*, even more caustic, on April 2. The *'Buss* contained an article about President Robert E. Vinson who was referred to as "Real-Issue Evader Vinson." The Faculty Discipline Committee suspended four prominent students, including the editor and managing editor of *The Daily Texan*, for the remainder of the term.

Nevertheless, in 1919 both papers appeared again. The *'Buss* revealed "improper relations between a named professor and one of his students. The issue also stated that Bolshevism was rampant in the law department. *The 'Bustle*, which appeared several hours after the *'Buss*, contained an editorial billed "The Answer":

> Let the censors snort and paw the air, even more so than last year. Let them summon the suspects, and with honeyed words, as last year, try to persuade them to confess or be kicked out of school. We know that old gag by now.

In spite of threats made by University, city, and county attorneys, *The Blunderbuss* or *The Blunderbustle*, or both, appeared in the Twenties every year, 1920 through 1924, and again in 1929. The Students' Assembly outlawed it, the Student Publications Board condemned it as "journalistic bushwhacking," but a student editor wrote, "The *Texan* rather hopes that there still remain a few of those students who are willing, as in the past, to take all risks in order that the school may learn the alleged 'truths' about its 'higher ups' on April 1."

In 1923, Travis County officers suppressed *The Blunderbuss* on the basis that an article not written by a University professor was attributed to him. Some 3,000 copies of the paper, which contained attacks on President Vinson, Dean Newton, and F. W. Graff, assistant to the President, were burned. A former student gave investigators the names of students who aided him and his brother to publish the paper. The case was turned over to the Men's Honor Council, but charges against the editors were dismissed on the request of President Vinson.

By 1924, copies sold for 25 cents. Editors found that getting copy was easy. All that was necessary was to publish exaggerated stories of indiscreet actions, parties, fights, and rumors of University staff squabbles, and the paper would sell. Names were slightly disguised so that they were recognizable. Athletes and popular students usually received more publicity than others. The sales had to be timed so that all could be sold within a short time before policemen could arrive on the scene. Some students profited by the popularity and scarcity of the papers. They would buy several papers and sell them later at a higher price.

After a five-year absence of the unofficial publication, the 'Buss appeared again on April 1, 1929. This one contained a sex questionnaire that had been suppressed at the University of Missouri. Eight men, one a high school student and a few University students, were arraigned in justice of the peace court for publishing the eight-page "dirty" sheet. Intensive investigation by city officials and the Dean of Men revealed that the paper was published in a downtown printing shop that had been rented for a Sunday for the purpose.

The Blunderbuss appeared again in 1930 and in 1933. The papers were far less controversial than earlier issues had been. The 1933 edition, "neither anonymous nor indecent," appeared the day before student elections and was an expose of campus politics. Because it was an unauthorized publication, the editor was suspended by the Faculty Discipline Committee.

ROUND-UP

In March, 1930, an invitation went out from the Ex-Students' Association to former students: Come home to the campus in April. On April 11, 12, and 13, the First Annual Round-Up of ex-students, mothers, dads, and friends of the University was held. William L. McGill was general chairman. A pageant, "Through the Years," was one of the highlights of the celebration. The Girl's Glee Club, the Men's Glee Club, the Curtain Club, the Texas Cowboys, the Longhorn Band, the American Legion Drum and Bugle Corps, the University Cavalry Troop, the men's and women's physical training departments, and other campus organizations participated. At the climax of the pageant, the first "Sweetheart of Texas," Myrtle Daunoy, was presented, and sweethearts of Baylor, T.C.U., Rice, S.M.U., and A. & M. were introduced; 280 Bluebonnet Belle nominees participated in the presentation. The pageant and ball that followed were held in the newly opened Gregory Gymnasium, the first unit completed in the University Union Building Program. The first revue marked its dedication. A student editor of The Daily Texan described the pageant:

> As the curtain arose upon the opening scene, Cowboys in costumes of orange shirts, black hats and yellow chaps were grouped around a campfire singing "Rounded Up In Glory," as they awaited the appearance of Texas' Sweetheart, who was expected home from college with a group of friends. Myrtle Daunoy, vivid in a pink tulle dress, arrived at her home on the ranch.

A song, written by Virginia Decherd and Alfina Ventresca for the sweetheart and sung for the first time that night over KUT by Florence Weymouth, was intended for the presentation but was not finished in time for orchestration. Words of the song were:

She's the Sweetheart of Texas U,
The girl of our dreams come true;
She's all a sweetheart can be—
A sweet sweetheart, you see,
For everybody knows,
She's just like a rose
The girl of our dreams come true,
The sweetheart of Texas U.

Various groups planned special social affairs for Round-Up. Fraternities, sororities, dormitories, and boarding houses, using western themes, decorated their houses. At one sorority party, supper was served in boxes at a counter in keeping with the country railroad station decorative motif. Fifty-five committees worked on plans for the first Round-Up. A profit of $2,002.30 was turned over to the Ex-Students' Association to form a revolving fund for preliminary expenses of future Round-Ups.

In spite of hard times of the Depression years, Round-Up was held each year and became the focal point for social activities. All during the Thirties, the Revue featured Janet Collet's musical extravaganzas. In 1931, sweetheart nominees and more than ninety candidates for Bluebonnet Belle honors wore cotton dresses for the presentation, as a Depression gesture. House decorations became more elaborate that year. Kappa Alpha Theta won first place in the sorority division for its one-ring circus and side show in front of the house. Action and noise were main features. Alpha Rho Chi won first in the fraternity group. Their front lawn was decorated as an old Spanish mission. A limit of twenty-five dollars was set on cost of decorations. Following the preliminary opening of the new women's gymnasium, the second unit of the Union Building Program, guests gathered on the banks of Waller Creek, west of the stadium, for an old-fashioned barbecue. More than one thousand were served.

The 1933 Round-Up was also the semicentennial celebration. Nine new buildings were dedicated. Robert Frost spoke, and a pageant, "Fifty Years on Forty Acres," was directed by James Parke.

The first Round-Up parade in 1934, with five floats, was the first student parade at UT in eight years. It was the beginning, however, of an annual tradition that climaxed in the late 1950's. The first parade offered tearful moments as floats stalled, took wrong turns, and began coming apart as fast as they could be put together.

In 1936, Alpha Tau Omega had the winning float. The theme was "100 Years of Progress," which depicted an old-fashioned saloon and a modernistic apartment, 1936 style, with a couple waiting for a mixed drink.

Loving cups were first awarded in 1938, but a Texas norther suddenly blew up during the parade, ripping the crepe-paper from the chicken wire floats.

The 1939 parade was labeled "the most elaborate of all time," with 77 floats taking part in the pomp and pageantry of the event. The floats were both clever and cynical. Phi Gamma Delta won Best All Around with its entry, which depicted the futility of war. The float showed a student receiving his diploma, joining the army, and being killed.

Before the 1940 parade plans started, Dean of Student Life, Arno Nowotny, issued a statement: "The Round-Up Parade has come to be recognized as the best college parade in the country; we've got to keep it that way." A meeting was held on the mall to urge campus groups to break the previous year's record of a 77-float parade.

In 1941, the parade rolled on as usual, despite the war. The "Reluctant Dragon," Alpha Chi Omega's entry, was considered the funniest by some viewers. The dragon with his tail of more than 60 feet, gave the viewers a riotous time. The half-concealed fellow who guided the tail had a difficult time making sharp turns and finally became separated from the dragon.

The parade was discontinued after 1941, because of the war but was resumed after 1946. The number of Belles was cut in 1944 to conserve paper for printing their pictures.

McArthur beer, anti-communism and comic-strip Humphrey were put together successfully in the 1948 parade. When one of the dignitaries leaned over the side of a long convertible and dropped his chewing gum in the street, the parade officially began.

By the mid-fifties, some organizations started complaining about the expense of the parade and wanted to stop having one. In 1958, the Central Round-Up Committee, by a vote of 8 to 3, temporarily ended the quarter-century tradition. The 1957 parade had been boycotted by many Greek groups who refused to build floats, but in 1958, with the University's 75th anniversary as the theme, the participating organizations gave what they thought would be the parade's final fling. But traditions aren't always killed by committees, and even though no parade was held in 1959, when Greek groups decorated their houses instead, one was started again in 1960. Only 14 floats were entered. In 1961, with Dr. Joseph Malik as chairman, the Central Round-Up Committee again voted to abolish the parade. Before World War II, a $25 limit was set on float expenditures. After the war, the amount was raised to $75, and in 1951, to $100. The next year, the limit jumped to $300. In 1954, $10,000 was spent by organizations on floats.

Until 1959, exhibits during Round-Up had been available in the various departments of the University, but in that year Round-Up told its story with displays in the Main Ballroom of the Texas Union. In 1960, "Showcase" boasted space-trained monkeys. Four years later the exhibits, costing $2,300 to $2,700 to light and set up, extended to the Union Junior Ballroom and the Star Room. By 1974, more than 70 areas of study were represented when former university engineers, who had distinguished themselves, were honored.

Fiscal responsibility became a big Round-Up issue in 1968. Fifty cents out of each Blanket Tax was allocated to the Central Round-Up Committee, and Assemblymen complained that $8,000 was being spent to bring three name bands to play at Round-Up dances. Interest in Round-Up declined in the late '60s and the event almost passed as a tradition in 1971. Cries of "irrelevant" during the turbulent, social-conscious years contributed to this near obliteration.

The parade was not held from 1960 until 1965, when it was cautiously revised, but a limit of $50 was placed on the cost of floats. Another crippling blow was dealt in 1967 when the Texas Relays were separated from the festivities.

In 1972, Round-Up passed from disinterested Student Government to the Interfraternity Council, and the spring activities returned to the campus. The parade was revised again, after a two-year absence, and seventeen floats, bicycles, the Shriner Band, and Smokey the Cannon moved from Municipal Auditorium up Congress to the Capitol. A group of anti-war protesters accompanied the parade, carrying such signs as "Free the Vietnamese" and passing out leaflets to parade watchers. Included among the events were a carnival on the West Mall, a baseball game, a concert, a barbeque, and a March-of-Dimes Marathon dance sponsored by the Silver Spurs in Gregory Gymnasium. Round-Up began with a Sun-

114

day afternoon street dance and a torch run from Mount Bonnell to the UT campus. Sponsors hailed the celebration as an "astounding success" as the 48-hour dance marathon netted $15,000 for the March-of-Dimes and the 2-day carnival netted about $1,000 in donations. Expenditures of the Interfraternity Council were estimated at approximately $500.

In 1973 and in 1974, Showcase, the parade, the carnival, and the dance marathon highlighted the week, which again opened with a torch run from Mount Bonnell. The parade each year featured approximately 25 units, mostly bands and floats.

A *Texan* editor, in 1973, captured the spirit of this continuing spring rite:

> Round-Up is more than a raucous week-end overflowing with beer, drunks, and dancing . . . for each there is in Round-Up what they want to find, just as there is at the University an answer to everyone's quest. For Round-Up symbolizes the University and the University is the culmination of man and his achievements, his interests and his involvements.

SCHOLZ'S

Although not located on the campus, Scholz Garten has been the rendezvous of generations of University students. Opened in 1866 by August Scholz as a place where Austin's German community could gather, eat, drink, and sing, it is still at its original location—1607 San Jacinto. Scholz operated the "garten" until his death in 1891, when ownership passed to his stepson, who managed it for a few years. The Lemp Brewery then bought it. In 1914, a German singing group, the Austin Saengerrunde, bought it and has owned it since that time, but it has been operated under a lease agreement in recent years.

Students are drawn to Scholz's by its relaxed and informal atmosphere. Seated at tables under oak trees with a pitcher of beer, exam-exhausted scholars enjoy its solace.

More graduate students can be counted at Scholz's on any Thursday night than the library can boast. It is

said that the Cowboys gather there to plan their annual fund-raising events. Without fail, the "Bored Martyrs" will fill the longest table in the place on a given day of the month. The Law School fraternities have even held their rush parties in front of the old, dark oak bar.

The atmosphere of the place has changed little during the years. It is still a melting pot of University students, Austinites and politicians. It is just what it has always been—an old German beer hall. On the walls hang many mementos of the past. On the bar, now an antique, is a huge German beer mug donated by one of Scholz's patrons and guaranteed to quench even the largest Texan thirst. It holds 2,172 ounces of brew! Along the paneled walls are pictures of every Longhorn football team since U. T.'s first undefeated season in 1893 when that great squad celebrated its victory there.

Finding his way to Scholz's is a part of every Tea-Sip's education!

EEYORE'S BIRTHDAY PARTY

On a hummy sort of day in the spring of 1964, Lloyd W. Birdwell, Jr. (Class of '64) was relaxing at the Delta Tau Delta house when a friend, John Hughes, asked, "Do you know what today is?" Lloyd answered without thinking at all, just as Christopher Robin in *Winnie-the-Pooh* would have done, "It's Eeyore's birthday party." (Eeyore was the Great Grey Donkey in A. A. Milne's book.) So that's how the custom began.

Lloyd thought of Eeyore at that moment because Eeyore and Pooh and Piglet and all their friends, even the newcomers to the forest, Kanga and Little Roo, had become popular with several sorority girls who were dating Delts that spring. The characters' names had become well known around the Delt house.

Lloyd and his friend, John, decided to give Eeyore a birthday party. It was scheduled for May 8, 1964, in Eastwoods Park. The ten founders were Lloyd and John and their friends—Dan Craddock, Judye Galeener, Judy Jordan, Susan Kline, Sally Lehr, John Mims, Larry Smith, and Susan Shaw. They each put up $10.00 for beer and decorations. Lloyd, being the best friend of Eeyore, put up the rest of the amount needed to pay the bills.

Invitations were printed and sent to people who should attend. One year the invitations were scrolls with the seal of the University in the shape of a donkey. According to Byron Cain, who has written the history of the custom for *Pearl*, Governor John Connally was invited but did not come. Senator Ralph Yarborough did attend and even wrote poems for Eeyore. Mrs. Lady Bird Johnson and Lynda attended in 1966.

The second year the party grew. Dr. James Ayres of the University's English Department became Eeyore's next best friend. Lloyd and his friend, Jean Craver, brought Dr. Ayres a Batman poster and asked him to be a sponsor. He has been one ever since.

The sponsors work very hard getting ready for the party. They work so hard that they are often unable to participate in the Event itself, but they have fun creating a party atmosphere for the guests.

The date of the Event changes every year, but Eeyore doesn't mind as long as he has a party. Lloyd has said that everyone in the world knows Eeyore's birthday is celebrated on April 11 and that the rain date is a week later, April 18. Only once has it rained. That was the year the Event went in the red. But, according to historian Cain, nobody really knows the budget anyway. The guests all pay $1.00 at the Edge of the Wood to help cover the expenses. The sponsors— some 25 or 30 now—each put up money to cover the pre-party costs.

The Event has grown so big that in 1974, after the City Parks Department and ecology groups noted trampled grass in Eastwoods Park, it was moved to Pease Park. Anyone who attends this party in the Other Part of the Forest must wear a costume. A maypole is always available, and of course a birthday cake is provided, but the guests are the main attraction. Eeyore likes it that way. The founders conceived the party as "a time for people of all different types to come together in a completely unpretentious, totally open and relaxed situation. No one is a teacher or a student or a businessman. They are all simply friends of Eeyore's."

SUNFLOWER CEREMONY

In the fall of 1900, senior class members considered the possibility of wearing caps and gowns for graduation. No one thought to send downstairs in the old Main Building, where the Law School was then located, to invite some Law seniors or some representative from the Law Department to the meeting. The Law students then met and decided they would not wear caps and gowns. Even though judges had worn the wig and gown for centuries, it was worn for a purpose entirely distinct from the purpose here proposed, they reasoned.

A decision was reached that Law students must conform to the wishes of the senior class or they must wear a significant insignia at Commencement. The Law students decided to wear Prince Albert coats and silk hats and sunflowers, picked from thousands growing near the campus, pinned on their lapels. The decision to wear sunflowers was not made in a spirit of conciliation or in appreciation for the dignity of the occasion. The students cited no reasons to justify their choice. The sunflower, or genus *Helianthus*, belongs to a family with world-wide distribution. "So do the lawyers," a *Texan* editor once wrote. "As the sunflower always keeps its face turned to the sun, the lawyer turns to the light of justice." In subsequent years senior men in the Law classes chose to wear white or light suits and senior women wore white or light dresses. The sunflower has never been abandoned.

The Sunflower Ceremony is held on Commencement Day twice each year and is attended only by senior Law students and their nearest relatives and friends. Originally, the sunflower was pinned on the coat lapel of each senior by his best friend. Today the Associate Dean of the Law School does the pinning.

COMMENCEMENT

On June 14, 1884, Dr. Ashbel Smith, first president of the Board of Regents, awarded a law degree to Richard Andrews, the first graduate of the University. At that first Commencement, thirteen students received law degrees and large bouquets of flowers.

The first bachelor of arts degree from the University was awarded to S. C. Red, the only member of the academic class of 1885.

Oratory, long and dull for many, gave political leaders and aspiring politicos opportunities to speak to a large audience. Austin is usually hot in June, and in the days before air conditioning, those attending Commencement ceremonies were often uncomfortable.

During the early years, Commencement Week was filled with social events. Fraternities planned special parties, literary societies closed the year with a big debate, and musical groups entertained students and visitors. Commencement Week at the turn of the century became a period of frivolity for students and one of deep concern for the faculty. One writer said that merry-making was generally felt to be more than the participants were able to bear. Moreover, the cost of the parties became prohibitive. The final ball took on more importance than graduation itself. The faculty finally took measures to limit the extent of social activities.

Until 1901, the custom of presenting flowers to speakers and to members of the graduating classes was observed. The custom became disturbing as classes became large and as some members had many flowers and others had none at all.

Typical of one of the early commencements, even after faculty had regulated the number and extent of social events, was that of 1913, "two days of crowd-appealing events, the most memorable celebration ever staged in Austin." More than 800 souvenir-badged alumni were registered. The entire city was draped in orange and white, and myriads of electric lights illuminated it. A 20-foot electric star hung from the tower of the old Main Building. Two bands gave concerts each night, and at a huge barbecue 2000 persons consumed 20 beefs, 15 sheep, 1200 loaves of bread, 50 pounds of butter, a barrel of dill pickles, 100 pounds of coffee, and 25 gallons of milk. A mammoth parade, "a splendid pageant two miles in length with 258 decorated cars," passed through the campus down Congress Avenue. Almost anticlimactic was the presentation of diplomas to 282 graduates.

The social glamour of Commencement lessened as the years passed. The U. T. faculty first wore academic regalia in 1905 because students complained that "various co-mingling of styles is not in accordance with the formality of the occasion." They did not continue to wear caps and gowns every year until after 1926. In that year, the graduation exercises were held in the new Memorial Stadium, which was "brilliantly illuminated and amplifiers this year enabled the seven thousand spectators to follow the ceremonies."

In recent years, U. T. graduates have been recognized at separate programs held by each college and school on Commencement Day. An interfaith baccalaureate service is held on the campus in the morning; that night a general Commencement program is held on the South Mall in front of the Main Building. At the program, each Dean certifies and presents the list of graduates from his college or school. Only recipients of doctoral degrees are personally recognized, as each is hooded by the Vice President and Dean of Graduate Studies. A representative of the

Board of Regents gives the President of the University the authority to confer degrees, which he or she does to all graduates at once.

As soon as degrees are conferred, the orange lights of the tower are turned on. Some prominent individual then addresses the graduates, everybody sings "The Eyes of Texas," and the Commencement program ends. Approximately 4,200 graduated in May, 1974, when U. T. graduate Alan Bean, the fourth man on the moon, addressed the class.

THE U. T. SENIOR RING

Seniors bought University rings for the first time in the spring of 1927. The ring was of 10-carat gold and had a garnet stone. The men's ring cost $13.00 and the women's ring was $10.50 at the time.

It was designed by Mrs. Darrell Jackson, technician in the Department of Zoology. The ring was described in *The Daily Texan:*

> On one shank appears a Longhorn head with a lariat draped from one horn around under the nose and up to the other horn. The number "27" is just above the head, and a lone star is just below the nose. In a semicircled wreath below the star is a group of Texas cacti. On the other shank is the degree and crest with a scroll bearing the words "Disciplina Praesidium Civitatis." Corresponding to the cacti on the first shank is a wreath of bluebonnets.

Today rings are available in a wide variety of styles, with or without stones, at most jewelry stores in Austin and at bookstores near the campus.

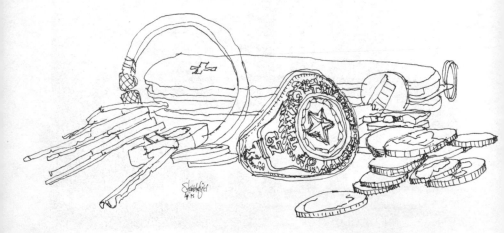

AUSTIN AND
THE HILL COUNTRY

The scenic and historical spots around Austin have provided students a backdrop and setting for social and recreational events through the years. Some of the retreats are as symbolic to University students as are the Tower or Littlefield Fountain.

Picnickers and nature lovers have looked for secluded places in the Austin hills. Sunset Ridge, Clover Fields, Mount Bonnell, Bull Creek, Lake Austin, and Hamilton's Pool have attracted numerous students. Mount Bonnell, associated with the legend of the Indian princess who jumped into the river in remorse over the death of her white lover—killed by her tribe to prevent their marriage—was a favorite place for picnics and is still a favorite symbol of environmentalists.

When, in 1915, a property owner fenced the road to Mount Bonnell, an ex-student wrote:

> I favor conservation of all of our influences for joy and affection and pleasure in life. At whatever cost, the Mount Bonnell road must be re-opened and at once. West Point has its 'Flirtation Walk'; Harvard has its own peculiar institutions and customs; Wisconsin has its lake; and Texas must have its Mount Bonnell. Without Mount Bonnell, it were as well for the University to close its doors. Presidents may change; governors may veto appropriations; Legislatures may be short-sighted and voters may be prejudiced; but never, never can we allow private greed to take away from The University of Texas its Mount Bonnell.

Boating, even in the days before motor boats, was also popular. Students used flat-bottomed boats and canoes, and they were occasionally lucky enough to have a houseboat. In recent years, water skiing and sailing have become year round sports. Some students own their own boats and spend week-ends on the lakes near Austin.

Swimming at Barton Springs and Deep Eddy have provided another diversion. In more recent years, Hippie Hollow on Lake Travis has been popular for skinny dipping. The swimming season is usually long in Austin, especially at Barton's, where the water remains the same temperature throughout the year.

Spots within Austin have also provided retreats for students. Waller Creek, Pease Park, Wooldridge Park, East Woods, Town Lake, and Shoal Creek are still some of the favorite places. A quotation from the 1918 *Cactus* might well be reprinted in the current issue:

> Rains have come and Austin is again the greenest place in the state. The mesquite, cedars, hackberries, post oak, live oak, elm, and all the other trees put forth their individual shades of green. It is the pleasant loafing season, and the campus is littered with loafers stretched out on the grass or lounging on the campus seats. The air, especially in the evenings and in the early mornings, is heavy with the scent of blooming locusts and orchard trees. Pansy beds are vying with each other in showing their brightest colors, and, of course, the mockingbirds are singing daytime and moonlight night. Indeed, Austin is a pleasant place. . . .

INDEX

A

Aggie Bonfire — 86-87
Alexander Fredericke Clair — 88
Allred, James V. — 74
Alma Mater, The — 23
Alpha Chi Omega — 112
Alpha Lambda Delta — 75, 76
Alpha Phi — 50
Alpha Phi Omega — 63, 64, 76
Alpha Rho Chi — 111
Alpha Tau Omega — 112
Alumni Center, Lila B. Etter — 25
Anderson, David — 41
Anderson, Tom — 41
Andrews, Richard — 121
Anniversary, Seventy-Fifth — 77
AstroTurf — 85
Athletic Council — 33, 35, 47, 87
Austin — 51, 125
Available Fund, University — 29
Ayres, James — 118

B

B. Hall — 67. 93
Band, Longhorn — 26, 53, 61, 72, 73, 74, 110
Barton Springs — 126
Battle Oaks — 56
Battle, William J. — 16, 17, 40, 57, 65
Bean, Alan L. — 25
Beck, Harry Birk — 55
Beck's Lake — 55
Bellmont, L. Theo — 83
Benedict, Harry Yandell — 80, 40, 25
Bertha, Big (Drum) — 61
Bevo — 30-37
Bewley, Lula Mary — 71
Billy Goat Hill — 48, 49
Birdwell, Lloyd W. — 118
Black, Hulon W. — 17, 20
Blanket Tax — 102, 114
Blocker, J. R. — 41
Blount, Edward A. Jr. — 19
Bluebonnet Belles — 106, 110, 111
Bluebonnet Chain — 71-77
Blunderbuss, The — 107-109
Blunderbustle, The — 108
Boner, Paul —40
"Bored Martyrs" — 117
Boyett, Jack — 34
Boyett, Lynwood — 34
Boyett, W. A. — 34
Brackenridge, George W. — 51
Brandon, Arthur — 101
Bredt, Carl V. — 77
Briscoe, Dolph Jr. — 105
Buffington, T. B. — 30

Bull Creek — 125
Byrd, D. Harold — 61

C

Cactus, The — 19, 105-106
Cain, Byron — 118
Calendar, The — 102
Calhoun, James W. — 57
Campus League of Women
    Voters — 75
Cannon, Jim R. — 23, 24
Cap and Gown — 71-77
Carlton, Charles — 41
Carnes, Marion — 41
Chimes — 39, 40, 41
Christmas Carol Program — 101
Christmas Dinners — 79
Clark Field — 46-49, 51
Clark, Harley Jr. — 18
Clark, James Benjamin — 46, 79, 80
Class Day — 71
Clock — 39, 41
Clover Fields — 125
Co-Ed Assembly — 75
Colors, University — 19, 43
Commencement — 44, 71, 121-123
Connally, Tom — 81
Constitution, Texas (1876) — 28
Coppini, Pompeo — 95, 98
Cowboys, Texas — 21, 60, 76, 110, 117
Cret, Paul P. — 39, 95
Cromwell, Carl — 28
Crow, Proctor — 41
Curtain Club — 110

D

Darden, Mrs. Mary Lee Prather — 23
Daunoy, Myrtle — 110
Deckherd, Virginia — 110
Deep Eddy — 126
Delta Tau Delta House — 118
Devine, Thomas J. — 15
DeVall, Mrs. Charles — 17
Diamond-T Ranch — 34
Dillingham, H. N. — 59
Dillingham's Pasture — 59
DiNino, Vincent R. — 62. 63
Disch, Billy — 47, 49
Disch-Falk Field — 49
Dobie, J. Frank — 42, 98, 99
Drum — 61

E

East Woods — 126
Eckhardt, Carl J. — 43
Eeyore's Birthday Party — 118
Ex-Students' Association — 25, 34, 110, 111
Eyes of Texas, The — 22, 40, 73, 123

F

Fairchild, Mrs. I. D. — 40
Falk, Bibb — 49
Farabee, Ray — 76
Flag, Texas — 63
Fleming, Richard T. — 21
Flinn, Helen — 76
Flodine, James — 64
Ft. Griffin State Park — 36
Forty Acres — 51
Frank, D. A. — 46
Friars — 76
Frost, Robert — 112

G

Garrison, George P. — 80
Gill, Joe H. — 88
Girls' Glee Club — 110
Goo Roos — 68
Gregory Gymnasium — 110
Gustafson, Cliff — 48

H

Hamilton's Pool — 125
Hancock Opera House — 23
Hardin, John III — 37
Hart, James P. — 70
Hermes — 92
Hill Country — 125
Hippie Hollow — 126
Hippie, Madame Augusta — 50
Hogg, Will C. — 81
Hook 'em, 'Horns — 18, 78
Houston, David F. — 65
Hughes, John — 118
Hurt, George E. — 101
Hunnicutt, Walter — 26, 69

I

Interfraternity Council — 76, 115

J

Jacoby's Beer Garden — 88
Jackson, Mrs. Darrell — 124
Jeffers, Leroy — 29
Johnson, James L. — 25
Johnson, Lewis Sr. — 25
Johnson, Lewis — 23
Jones, J. S. (Snakey) — 81
Journalism, School of — 102
Junior Fellows — 77

K

Kappa Alpha Theta — 111
Key, Scott — 90
King, C. Richard — 80
King , James E. — 26
Kirby, Helen Marr — 107
Kivlehen, J. D. — 23
Klotz, Diana — 76
Kreisle, Leonardt F. — 17, 20
Krupp, Haymen — 27
Kuehn, Mrs. Flo — 64

L

Lake Austin — 125

Lamar, Mirabeau B. — 16
Law School — 120
Lights, Victory — 43-45
Littlefield, Clyde — 21
Littlefield, Fountain — 75, 95-98
Littlefield, George — 53, 95
Locklin, Dee — 28
Lockwood, Lee — 17
Long, Walter E. — 70
Longhorn, The — 105
Longhorns — 54

M

Malik, Joseph — 113
Marathon Dance — 114, 115
March 2 — 68, 81-82, 93
Marjorie Darilek Award — 76
Martinez, Rumiro — 41
McCall, Jim — 90
McClendon, James W. — 21, 81
McCrory, W. W. — 81
McCurdy, John — 34
McDonald, R. S. — 27
McGill, William L. — 84, 110
Memorial Stadium — 47, 83-85
Men's Co-Op Association — 76
Men's Glee Club — 110
MICA — 76
Mike Flynn Award — 76
Moeser, James — 41
Moody, Dan — 89
Moore, Paul — 41
Mortar Board — 73, 75, 76
Mount Bonnell — 114, 125
Moursund, A. N. — 81
Mustangs — 99

N

Neans, B. B. — 58
Neff, Patrick — 81
Newton, Frank R. — 81
Newton, Lucy J. — 71, 108
Weymouth, Florence — 110
Nostalgia, definition — 14
Nowotny, Arno (Shorty) — 112
Nunnally, Ed — 24

O

Ogden, Ralph R. — 99
Orange Jackets — 21, 75
Owen, Jim — 41

P

P.E.C.'s — 68
Panhellenic — 75
Pansy Bed — 52
Parade, Round-Up — 112-115
Parlin, H. T. — 74
Parten, S. R. — 36
Patron Saints — 88-92
Pease Park — 119, 126
Pennybacker, Mrs. Percy V. — 75
Peregrinus — 71, 90
Permanent Fund, University — 29

Perip — 53
Pharr, Burnett — 26
Phi Beta Kappa — 73, 75
Phi Eta Sigma — 76
Phi Gamma Delta — 112
Pickrell, Frank T. — 27
Pickney, Stephen — 30
Pitts, Henry — 18
Pope, Elmer — 90
Porter, Ralph A. — 23
Prather, William Lambdin 16, 23, 24
Prexy's Pot — 65
Price, Edwin — 76
Proctor, A. Phiminster — 99
Proctor, Venable B. — 19
Pushball Contest — 82, 93-94

R

Ragsdale, Smith — 15
Ranger, The — 102
Ransom, Harry — 21
Reagan County — 27
Red Candles — 50
Red Cross Fete of Nations — 72
Ricker, Rupert — 27
Red, S. C. — 121
Rigsby, Lee — 41
Ring, U. T. Senior — 124
Round-Up — 57,110-115
Row, Mrs. Martin A. — 75
Royal, Darrell — 21
Rusticusses — 68

S

St. Peter's Gate — 58
Santa Rita — 27-29
Schoch, E. P. — 70
Scholz's — 116-117
Scholz, August — 116
Schreiner, Charles — 35
Seal, University — 15
Searight, J. W. — 33
Shoal Creek — 126
Showcase — 113, 115
Silver Spur Cup — 76
Simkins, W. S. — 90
Sinclair, John Lang — 23
Smith, Ashbel — 15, 121
Smith, W. D. — 23
"Smokey " — 60, 114
Sparks, Sam — 84
Spurs, Silver — 35, 76, 114
Stark, H. J. Lutcher — 40, 83, 84
Still, Rae Files — 75
Students' Assembly — 32, 108
Suicides, Tower — 41
Sunflower Ceremony — 120
Sunset Ridge — 125
Sutton, Eldon — 41
Sweetheart of Texas — 110
Sweetheart Song — 111
Swing-Out — 71-77

T

Taylor, T. U. — 80
Tea-Sippers — 78, 117
Ten Most Beautiful — 106
Texan Oil and Land Company — 27
Texan, The Daily — 102-104
Texas A. & M. — 28, 36, 50, 86
Texas Fight — 26, 69
Texas Student Publications, Inc. — 102-104
Texas Union — 75, 113
Thompson, Joe C. (Jodie) — 77
Toombs, Alf — 88
Torch Run — 114, 115
Tower — 24, 39-45
Town Lake — 126
Townes, John C. — 46, 80, 89
Traditions, definition — 13, 77

U

Udden, John A. — 27
Underwood, H.W. — 74
UTSA — 75, 76

V

Ventresca, Alfina — 110
Vinson, Robert E. — 51, 108, 109

W

Waller Creek — 111, 126
Warner, Mrs. Robert W. — 75
Water Tank — 65
Webb, Walter Prescott — 29
Western Lands, University — 27
White, R. L. — 40
Whitman, Charles Joseph — 41
WICA — 75
Wilcox, William M. — 45
Wilson, Jerry — 76
Wilson, Logan — 17
Winston, George T. — 81, 82
Woman's Building — 47, 55
Wooldridge Park — 126

Y

Yantis, H.C. — 40
Yantis , Janet — 40
YMCA — 76
YWCA — 75
Young, Charles — 16

Z

Zeta Tau Alpha — 50

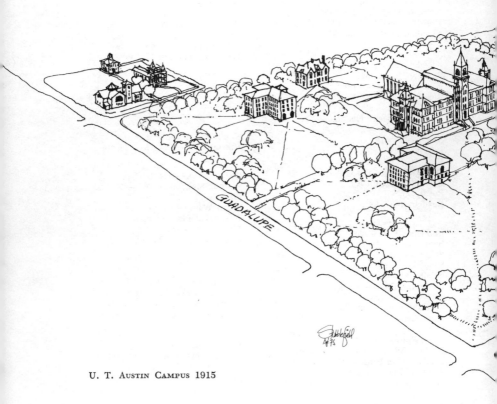

U. T. Austin Campus 1915

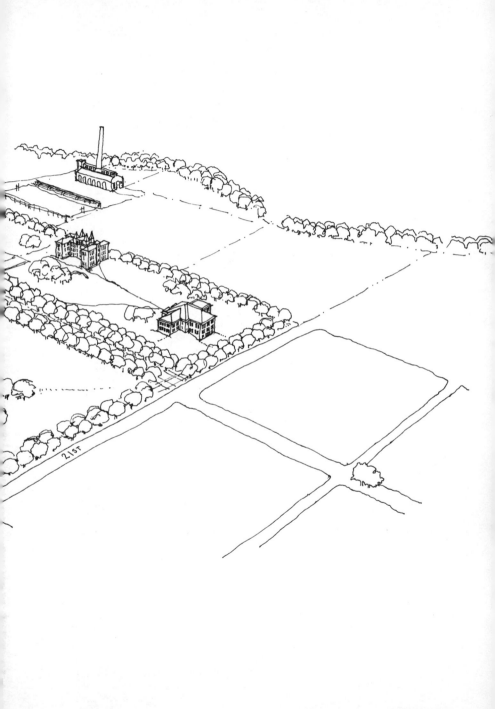